THE LITERATURE OF
DEATH AND DYING

THE LITERATURE OF
DEATH AND DYING

Advisory Editor
Robert Kastenbaum

Editorial Board
Gordon Geddes
Gerald J. Gruman
Michael Andrew Simpson

DISASTER

A Psychological Essay

Martha Wolfenstein

ARNO PRESS

A New York Times Company

New York / 1977

Reprint Edition 1977 by Arno Press Inc.

Copyright © 1957 by The Free Press,
    A Corporation
This edition is reprinted by arrangement
    with The Free Press, A Division of
    Macmillan Publishing Co., Inc.

Reprinted from a copy in
    The Pennsylvania State Library

THE LITERATURE OF DEATH AND DYING
ISBN for complete set: 0-405-09550-3
See last pages of this volume for titles.

Manufactured in the United States of America

———◆———

Library of Congress Cataloging in Publication Data

Wolfenstein, Martha, 1911-
    Disaster.

    (The Literature of death and dying)
    Reprint of the ed. published by the Free Press,
Glencoe, Ill.
    Includes bibliographical references.
    1. Disasters--Psychological aspects. I. Title.
II. Series.
BF789.D5W6 1977   155.9'35   76-19595
ISBN 0-405-09589-9

DISASTER:

A Psychological Essay

DIS

A Psychological Essay

THE FREE PRESS
GLENCOE, ILLINOIS

&

 THE FALCON'S WING PRESS

ASTER

by *Martha Wolfenstein*

Library of Congress Catalog No. 57-6752

Contents

Introduction . . . . *x*

Acknowledgments

THIS BOOK is the result of a study undertaken for the Committee on Disaster Studies of the National Academy of Sciences-National Research Council. The Committee's support was provided from funds supplied by a grant from the National Institute of Mental Health, Public Health Service, Department of Health, Education and Welfare. Harry Williams, Jeannette Rayner, and Charles Fritz of the Committee on Disaster Studies were extremely helpful in providing me with materials and sharing with me their extensive knowledge of the field. The conference organized by the Committee at Vassar College in February 1955 raised many relevant questions and offered numerous insights.

I received much valuable stimulation from discussions with Margaret Mead and Irving Janis and am grateful for their suggestions about the manuscript. I am also very grateful to Charlotte Roland for the interviews which she conducted in Paris in June 1955 on reactions to the catastrophe at the racetrack of Le Mans. Many of the ideas and the clarification of many points in this study I owe to the tireless interest, devoted help, and perennial cleverness of Nathan Leites.

Introduction

IT IS NOT EASY to find out how disasters affect people. In the best of times our observations of human nature are rather rarely intensive or systematic. In the alarm, disorder, pain and grief created by large scale catastrophes, there have been too many more urgent things to do. It is only recently that research teams have been going into the field to interview victims of disasters, and to observe some of the consequences of such events. The present study is based on material collected in this way, mainly from peace-time disasters in the United States. The material on which I have worked has been brought together by the Committee on Disaster Studies of the National Research Council, and the central core of the data consists of protocols of tape-recorded interviews with disaster victims, gathered by research teams of the National Opinion Research Center of the University of Chicago, the Disaster Research Project of the Psychiatric Institute of the University of Maryland, and the Waco-San Angelo Disaster Study of the Department of Sociology of the University of Texas.

I have taken these data as a basis for formulating a series of hypotheses about how people react to disastrous events. For this purpose I have attempted to apply hypotheses derived from psychoanalysis to material which is suggestive but non-intensive and fragmentary. For the testing of the hypotheses which I present much more intensive observation would be required. Since this study was undertaken as a contribution to further research planning, let me indicate in a general way the kinds of statements with which I am concerned and the kinds of additional data which they call for.

1. I have tried to describe and interpret a range of subjective and behavioral phenomena which occur in people involved in a disaster. However, this is often based on very rough and summary descriptions. Take, for instance, what has been called the "disaster syndrome." People who have just undergone the impact of an extreme event may describe themselves, or be described by others as "shocked," "stunned," or "dazed." I have tried to reconstruct in a conjectural way the inner dynamics of this state. But the subjective content of the state itself has as yet been only very incompletely reported. The same applies to the illusion of invulnerability which some individuals are supposed to be able to preserve in moments of extreme danger while others lose it. We need much more precise and detailed descriptions of these and other subjective states which as yet remain obscure.

2. I have elaborated a number of dynamic hypotheses to account for various reactions to disaster. For instance, I have suggested that the upsurge of loving feelings towards others following a disaster is related to a surfeit of vicarious gratification of hostile impulses by the extensive damage which has been done. The predominance of good sentiments may thus be considered as in part a consequence of the temporary subsidence of the negative feelings which at other times interfere with them. Or, I have suggested that the humility sometimes expressed by survivors, the resolve to lead better lives, may be motivated by the need to defend oneself against the sin of pride. One may be tempted to feel superior in one's immunity (of course nothing can happen to me). But this may be followed by alarm that the powers that be will punish one for such presumption. The danger is then warded off by a submissive and dutiful attitude. (Needless to say,

in the case of these reactions and others I have envisaged a multiplicity of alternative or mutually reenforcing motives.) However, it is clear that for the confirmation of any such dynamic proposition more intensive data would be required than are at present available.

3. For every phase of a disastrous experience I have indicated a considerable range of possible reactions. There are some people, for example, who ignore warnings of an oncoming disaster, while others pay attention to them. Following a disaster, there are some people who talk about it continuously while others cannot bear to hear it mentioned. Many people move back again into a disaster-stricken area and reestablish their homes on the same ground. But there are some who move away. Again, after a disaster, some survivors feel, 'I must be pretty good, a favorite of the gods, or I would not have survived.' Others in the same situation are overwhelmed with guilt, feeling that they should have sacrificed themselves for loved ones who perished. In the case of these and any number of other alternative reactions, the question arises: what are the conditions for their occurrence? Who will react one way and who another? It is of course particularly important to try to determine the conditions for recovery from a disastrous experience and the conditions under which it may leave more or less lasting disturbances. On the basis of general clinical knowledge, I have speculated about some of the factors which may be operative in such alternative ways of reacting. Again, such hypotheses would need to be checked by much more information than we now have about individuals who react in these various ways.

4. While we may be able to indicate something of the range of possible reactions before, during, and after a disastrous event, we still do not know about the combinations of such reactions or their frequencies. At the end of Part II (in the section on Activity and Emotion) I sketch sequences of feelings and behavior throughout the course of a disaster as reported by two exceptionally articulate and self-observant subjects. But even in these cases the information is very fragmentary. On the whole we cannot as yet identify recur-

rent combinations and sequences of reactions. Of the various attitudes expressed by different people following a disaster, we cannot say which usually go together or what is the interplay between them. For instance, many people following a disaster are tormented by the memory of it. Also many people stress how lucky they were to escape with less damage than others. Sometimes the same people express both these attitudes. But I cannot say what the interplay is between the distress about the terrible experience which one cannot forget and the feeling of having been so lucky. Nor do I know how often one of these attitudes occurs in the absence of the other. Thus I describe and interpret a series of attitudes but I do not have enough material on individual subjects to present a series of combinations of reactions. To take a more complicated instance, I consider denial or acknowledgment of danger as it occurs in four phases of a disastrous event: when it is in the remote future, when it is imminent, in the moment of impact, and after it has passed. I attempt to indicate at which points denial is or is not pathological and/or pathogenic. However, there are sixteen possible combinations of denial and non-denial for these four phases. I have no detailed exemplification of any one of these possibilities, let alone any basis for estimating their relative frequencies. Even apart from the question of combinations or sequences of reactions, there are very few points where separate items of feeling or behavior have been quantified (as in the predominant tendency to be unworried about remote threats, and to move back into a disaster-stricken area). All the ways of acting and feeling which I describe and the underlying motives which I suggest may be supposed to occur in some people at some times and in some places. But the question of frequencies, like that of conditions, remains to be decided.

I have at various points ventured interpretations in cultural terms of various reactions which I have found recurrent in my material. So, for instance, in the emphasis on keeping calm, and in the repeated assertion "we were lucky" despite whatever damage or losses were suffered, I have been inclined to see something characteristically American. Similarly, the extremity of guilt of some of the survivors at Nagasaki, the feeling that they should have died in the attempt, however futile, to save their loved ones, seemed related to certain distinctive traits of Japanese culture. These judgments of what may be culturally distinctive are based on the coherence of the reactions observed in disasters with other attitudes which, in previous studies of the given cultures, have appeared to be characteristic of them. Such cultural hypotheses would again require much more extensive observations for their verification. To affirm cultural regularities, of course, in no way precludes acknowledgment of the wide range of individual differences, of other group differences, nor of commonly human responses. As an instance of the latter, I believe that the view of disaster as the great equalizer (the high are made low) is, if not universal, at least very widely recurrent.

While the hypotheses which I present are intended as suggestions for further research, they would also require a more precise reformulation for this purpose. So, for instance, with the hypothesis about the reduction of hostility as a condition for altruistic feelings and behavior following a disaster: it would be necessary to develop indices of the degree of increase of altruistic sentiments and activity and of the degree of reduction of hostility in order to test this hypothesis. Similarly with the other hypotheses here presented, they would have to be translated into operational language. I have not attempted to do this at this point. Rather I have tried to give the emotional flavor of the experiences of disaster victims in what aims to be an evocative and empathic way.

I have been largely occupied with reconstructing motives which are unconscious or not fully conscious. This, however, does not mean that I am mainly concerned with non-adaptive behavior. Unconscious motives may lead to useful undertakings or may reenforce consciously reality-oriented activities. So, for instance, thinking about and preparing precautionary devices against a future disaster may be in some degree motivated by the need to master the trauma of a past one. Consciously the individual may be concerned with the physical efficacy of these precautions. Less consciously he may be working over his unresolved feelings of alarm from the disastrous experience already undergone. Also, on a less conscious level, precautions may be invested with a power of prevention. Thus I am concerned here with underlying as well as manifest motives for all kinds of reactions to disaster, with no special emphasis on psychiatric casualties.

In his book on *Air War and Emotional Stress*, Irving Janis summed up what had been learned about reactions of civilians to the bombing of cities in World War II. It is not necessary here to recapitulate all of those findings. The present study concentrates on recently gathered material from peace-time disasters. However, I have drawn on observations of war-time reactions of citizens and soldiers to supplement and fill in gaps in this latter material. To delimit further the scope of this report, I have not undertaken to deal with the functions of social organizations in coping with disasters, and in the range of reactions of individuals I have not attempted to investigate psychosomatic disturbances.

In relating what I have been able to find out or surmise about how people react to disasters I have followed a simple time sequence: the first part deals with the phase before a disaster, the second with its impact and the time immediately following, and the third with the aftermath. However, since I have tried to make connections as far as I can between later and earlier events, there is a certain amount of looking before or after in each part.

The first part begins with remote dangers, the predominant tendency to be unworried about them even though they may be considered probable, and the subjective conditions which make some people alarmed about them. I then consider some of the prognoses about large-scale disasters put forward by those who are forced to anticipate such events, and particularly expectations of mass panic and madness. There follows a consideration of denial of imminent threats and the consequences of such denial; attitudes about precautions and efforts at propitiation of fate; some of the ways in which past experience of catastrophe influences anticipations; and the effects of sharing danger with others. Recent peace-time disasters on which research has been done have been mainly of a sudden and unexpected sort (such as tornadoes). So for the discussion of attitudes towards a threat which is recognized in advance I have drawn to a considerable extent on observations made in Britain during the bombings in the last war. It is in parts two and three that the material from recent interviews with disaster victims becomes the major data for analysis.

In part two, I discuss the impression of the disaster victim in the moment of impact that he alone has been hit, or that the destructive force is focused on the spot where he is, and the painful feeling of having been abandoned by both human and superhuman sources of help. I then attempt to analyze the conditions under which the individual's sense of invulnerability is shattered or preserved in an experience of extreme danger, the near-miss and remote-miss reactions. There is then a discussion of the dynamics of the disaster syndrome, the state in which the person who has just undergone an extreme event appears stunned and dazed. This is followed by a consideration of panic, the different meanings of the term, the conditions for the occurrence of various kinds of panic, and some speculation about why the extreme form of panic appeals so strongly to the imagination (to account for its being anticipated so much more often than it happens). I then discuss the altruistic behavior which is often so marked immediately following a disaster, as well as tendencies towards orgiastic abandon which are sometimes manifested in extreme situations. This part concludes with a consideration of divergent tendencies toward emotional excitement or efficient action, and of alternations between distressed and euphoric feelings in living through a catastrophe.

In the third part I consider the repeated revival of a traumatic experience in memory, and efforts to ward off such painful recollections. I take the occasion to bring together the hypotheses about the conditions and effects of denial in the various phases of a disaster. I discuss the expectations of an imminent recurrence of a catastrophe on the part of those who have undergone it. There follows an account of the great attraction which a disaster locale has for sightseers coming in from outside, and the variety of motives which impel disaster victims to move back into the same area. Next I proceed to examine the sentiment expressed by survivors that they do not regret the loss of their property (property being regarded as a payment for life), and that they are very lucky, despite whatever damage they have suffered: it is someone else rather than themselves who should be pitied. I then attempt to interpret the rise of strong positive feelings for others immediately following a disaster, and the subsequent decline of these good feelings. Finally I consider issues often raised by a disaster as to whether men or gods are to blame, and the alternatives of revolt against the powers that be or submission to them in the face of catastrophe.

Part I:
Threat

I.

Who worries about remote dangers?

HUMAN LIFE is liable to many hazards. People are run over in the street, automobiles collide, travelers are injured or killed in train wrecks or airplane crashes. In the seeming security of one's home one may fall down stairs and break a leg. A child playing hide and seek may close himself in an old ice box and suffocate. One may fall prey to disease or something may go amiss with a vital organ—a heart attack, a brain hemorrhage. The cocktails and cigarettes which we enjoy may be working irremediable internal damage. And then there are the more large scale dangers of fire, flood, earthquake, tornado, and the man-made destruction unleashed in war. As we consider such a list, is not our first reaction apt to be one of smiling? Yes, we will say, and as you are walking down the street a tile may fall from a roof and hit you on the head. But who can worry about all these things?

It is with this reaction that I should like to begin: the attitude of denial towards remote threats. This denial has a number of aspects or alternative forms. We may exclude various threats from awareness. We simply do not think about them. Or if we think about them, we do not believe that they will happen, or that they can affect us. Or even if

we entertain the possibility that they may affect us we take
this as a purely intellectual statement to which we attach
no feeling.

In considering reactions to disasters, I shall try to show
the varying role of denial in relation to different temporal
phases of a disastrous event: in relation to a remote threat,
to an imminent threat, to the impact of extreme danger, and
to the phase of retrospect. We shall see that the conditions
and consequences of denial vary with these different phases.

Certain attitudes towards a remote threat appear in the
findings of a survey made in 1946 of Americans' feelings and
forecasts about the atomic bomb.[1] Half of the subjects in this
nation-wide study said that they were not at all worried about
the bomb, while only one-eighth acknowledged being de-
cidedly worried; the rest were slightly worried. How was this
preponderance of non-worry related to prognoses about the
future? Few people felt confident that the bomb would not
be used against the United States. Thus absence of worry
frequently coexisted with acknowledgment of the danger.
The relative independence of worry and prognoses appears
further in the attitudes of more and less well informed individuals. Those who were better informed on world affairs
were less likely to believe that the bomb would work for
peace by making other countries afraid of the United States;
they were more ready to believe that other countries would
soon get the bomb (this was in 1946); and they were more
doubtful that the United States would find a means of
defense against the bomb. Yet they did not worry any more
than the less well informed who inclined to the opposite,
more optimistic prognoses.

One may ask: what is the state of mind of someone who
acknowledges the likelihood of such an extreme danger but
does not feel worried? I am reminded of another paradoxical
combination of feeling and belief, what Coleridge called "the
willing suspension of disbelief which constitutes poetic faith."
In this one responds to events in a story or on the stage with
strong emotion even while one knows they are not real. In
the opposite situation, a reality value is attached to an event

but without emotional response. This is the position of those who consider an atomic attack (or today, of course, it would be an H-bomb attack) against the United States likely, but do not feel worried. We have here what would appear to be an isolation of affect rather than the denial of an external situation. But does not the external situation which elicits no emotional response seem in some sense "unreal"? Is not the acknowledgment of it merely verbal? In *The Death of Ivan Ilyich,* Tolstoy describes how the dying man recalls the syllogism he learned in school, beginning with the general proposition: All men are mortal. While he had not doubted this proposition, still it had seemed to have no application to himself. Only now that he was faced with imminent death, this commonplace sentence became infused with meaning. Admission of a painful prospect on a purely verbal level may thus coexist with denial on a less conscious level, or with the implicit qualification: it does not apply to me.

Important factors in attitudes towards future dangers are estimates of whether anything can be done about them, and whether the individual himself is in a position to do anything. In respect to the bomb, the same survey indicated that expectations of its being used against the United States were frequently combined with the counteracting expectation that before this would happen the United States would have developed an adequate defense. This confidence that the "leaders" or the "government" could and would do something was generally combined with a belief that there was nothing the private citizen could do. Such attitudes towards world affairs illustrate the trend of what has been called "privatization."[2] The ordinary citizen tends to feel increasingly that he has neither the knowledge nor the means to take a hand in the great affairs which affect his destiny.

The association between non-worry and the conviction that there was nothing the individual could do was sometimes made quite explicitly. As one person put it: "It's just like living in a country where there were earthquakes. What good would it do if you went to bed every night worrying whether there would be an earthquake?"[3] The conviction that there is nothing one can do figured prominently also in the opinions of a smaller sample of subjects interviewed in 1950 on the prospects of nuclear bombing.[4] In this group, an expression of lack of worry tended to be coupled with doubts whether these weapons would ever be used. When the interviewer questioned such optimistic prognoses, interviewees showed some apprehension at the same time that they pictured a nuclear attack as a situation about which nothing could be done. According to their image, all within a certain radius would be killed, while all outside it would be safe. This evidently would make any preparation for post-attack remedial activities superfluous. Probably the conviction that nothing can be done and the oversimplified image of the event reenforced one another. While it was found that avoidance of anxiety and denial of danger tended to yield to the pressure of conflicting evidence put forward by the interviewer, one may suppose that his subjects ceased to think about his arguments after the interview was over. In dealing with a remote threat, denial is often not total. But it may be something that one thinks about only very rarely. And having taken the pains to think about it once, one may feel that one has paid the price of emancipation from this worry: one need not think about it again for quite a while.

Thus we see a number of the factors which affect attitudes towards a remote threat. There are varying estimates of the likelihood that the threat will materialize. One may or may not believe, for instance, that nuclear weapons will be used, or may assign varying degrees of probability to this prospect. One's belief in the likelihood of the danger may be purely verbal and may coexist with disbelief on a deeper level. One's acknowledgment of the dangerous possibility may be continuous or intermittent, alternating with implicit denial. One may more or less explicitly exempt oneself from possible involvement. Again, one may estimate variously the possibilities of preventive or remedial action. And one may have different ideas about whether one could oneself take any such action. Anxiety about a remote threat seems to be little related to prognoses. This suggests that the belief in the coming danger on the part of those who remain unworried is not very intense. The expectation that superior authorities will do something to ward off the threat, and the often combined belief that the individual himself can do nothing, are apt to be associated with absence of worry. In connection with remote threats, the usual reaction appears to be explicit or implicit denial that it will materialize or that it can apply to oneself, and isolation of affect from the idea of the event.

However, there are evidently some people, though a minority, who do worry about remote dangers. Who are they, and what factors account for their anxiety? Let us leave aside for the moment those whose position of authority and responsibility requires them to anticipate dangerous possibilities and consider those who worry on their own. There is considerable clinical evidence to suggest that those who are apprehensive about remote dangers, or more terrified than others about less remote hazards, are so not because of a more realistic attitude towards the world but rather on the basis of emotional factors. The individual's own impulses or fantasies of punishing agencies are projected on the external world. Take, for example, the situation in New York City during World War II, when there were regular air raid drills in the schools. For most of the participants apparently these drills were either a dull routine or a brief respite from chores, with little thought being given to the not very imminent danger to which they were related. Some children, however, and also some adults, became acutely anxious in this situation, with fears of bombs exploding and houses being blown to bits. A therapist in a child guidance clinic observed among patients who showed this reaction an emotional predicament which constituted the real though unrecognized danger. These were individuals who in their family relations experienced intense hostility together with great fear of retaliation if they expressed it. They felt that they would be precipitated into great danger if the hostility which they inhibited precariously and with great effort were to break through. This, then, was the explosion which they dreaded, the image of which became projected on the outer world. The danger of bombs exploding thus seemed imminent to them though it did not to others in the same external circumstances.[5] Similar factors operate to produce more than ordinary alarm in imminent danger situations. Thus the rare air-raid phobias observed in London during the last war appeared to be related to unconscious fantasies which were stimulated by the falling bombs.[6]

Comparing those who are fearful and those who are unworried about remote threats, we could advance the hypothesis that both construe the external world on the model of their internal emotional situations. The individual who fears that he may not be able to control his own destructive impulses anticipates on the basis of projection that explosive forces in the external world may break through restraining bonds. Conversely, those who remained unworried about the hazards of the atomic bomb frequently expressed confidence that their government would find a way to counteract its destructive force. The counterpart in terms of internal dynamics would be that in these subjects hostile impulses are sufficiently under the control of ego and super-ego that they do not fear being carried away by involuntary outbursts. Thus, in relation to remote threats, we may say that those who are relatively free from inner strain will not be likely to worry about them, and such worry when it occurs will usually indicate some emotional disturbance. This is not to say that everyone with emotional difficulties worries about possible world catastrophes. There are so many other things that the neurotic may worry about, which may even make him quite indifferent to, say, the dangers of bombing even when they are immediately present. In other morbid conditions there is a pervasive absence of emotion. We must distinguish between the lack of worry which is a manifestation of such an affectless state and that which derives from emotional well-being. And we should note that it is only in certain kinds of emotional disturbances, as yet not sufficiently delimited, that anxiety about world cataclysms becomes prominent.

There are many motives which may contribute to vivid

fantasies of future disaster, while the content of these fantasies is also subject to great variation. There are terrible and grandiose visions, like those in the Book of Revelation; there are cults whose members anticipate and prepare for the end of the world. Similarly, some pacifists, between the two wars, conjured up terrifying pictures of a future war as the end of mankind. They seemed to be possessed by apprehensions of the end of the world such as are often found in schizophrenics, who express in this way their frighteningly reduced capacity to attach any feeling to the outer world. In trying to impose their terrifying visions on others, they were impelled in part by sadistic motives.[7] Making others afraid also serves as a defense against one's own terror; one can feel: I dare to face it; it is they, not I, who are afraid. Combined with this there may also be a motive of restitution, an effort to save or restore the world which is in danger of disappearing.

Guilt feelings and fear of punishment may also stimulate apprehension of catastrophe. This is a major theme running through emotional reactions to all phases of disasters. There is a deep-lying tendency in human nature to take everything that happens as a reward or a punishment meted out by higher powers. The model for this view is the relation of the child to his parents. More particularly, children learn to deal with the dangers of the external world mainly through the mediation of parental protection, warning and punishment. On the whole they are not left to find out about the hazards of the physical world by direct experience, by trial and error. If they were, they would not survive to a very advanced age. Thus rules of safety and rules of obedience come to be inextricably intertwined. The child who crosses the street alone may be more afraid of mother's scolding, if she were to find out, than of the passing cars. But it is not only the child who feels this way. How many adults, for instance, in not complying with the doctor's orders feel, instead of worry about their health, glee at eluding authority or guilt for non-compliance. And the same thing happens, as we shall see in numerous instances, in the more obscure relations with the authorities who are felt to preside over events in the world at large. During the bombing of Britain, a woman who had been untroubled by anxiety all at once became intensely apprehensive. It turned out that she had just written a disagreeable letter to her mother.[8] Unconsciously, for her, the powers that were meting out life and death in war were identical with the punishing mother of her childhood.

Fear of death may express an unconscious expectation of talion punishment for death wishes towards others. Where an external danger situation exists it may readily be incorporated into a pre-existing fantasy of anticipated retaliation. In Britain during the last war, some of those who became neurotically preoccupied with bombing hazards had already previously suffered from fear of death because of guilt feelings. The external danger seemed to confirm their expectations of merciless justice.[9] Among patients who showed extreme fear of air-raids, some were observed who held themselves responsible for the death of a buddy during the first war.[10] For them a long-deferred punishment was about to be carried out.

Another emotional condition which conduces to extreme apprehensiveness is an initial reaction to the threat of danger by a withdrawal of emotional energy from external objects and an intensified concentration on the self. This manoeuver, unconsciously intended as protective, may work to the opposite effect. Alarm about the self is increased by absorption in oneself, following the same mechanism as that of hypochondriacal anxiety about an overly libidinized body part.[11] Conversely, strong attachment to others is a major protection against undue anxiety about the self. We shall see later how frequently this operates in reactions following a disaster.

2.

Visions of panic and madness

LET US NOW turn to anticipations of extreme events on the part of those who are required by positions of authority and responsibility to predict and prepare for such eventualities. Here the concern with danger would seem to be commanded by reality. We would expect less anxiety and a more serious attempt to arrive at a realistic picture than in those whose anticipations of catastrophe express private emotional concerns. However, where there are no exact precedents, gaps must be filled in by inference and imagination. And here the way is opened for the emergence of various latent fantasies.

It is well known how much the predictions of government agencies and consulting experts in Britain before the last war differed from the subsequent events. It had been widely assumed in these groups that if London were bombed great masses would flee the city in panic; that psychiatric casualties would outnumber physical casualties at the rate of three to one; that the death rate per ton of bombs would be three or more times what it actually turned out to be. On the other hand, destruction to houses was very incompletely anticipated. In the actual event, for every citizen killed, thirty-five were bombed out of their homes.[12]

Not only was the mortality rate greatly overestimated in

the forecasts, but the anticipated mass flight of terrified city
dwellers and the tremendous onset of madness did not materialize. Let us recall that the prognoses were in this case
concerned with a largely unknown situation. A bombing
"capability" comparable to Germany's in 1940 had never
been fully used. The British authorities and experts may have
wanted to prepare for the worst. In this way one not only
attempts to provide oneself with the necessary facilities, but
one inures oneself emotionally, one wards off the danger of
being overwhelmed by the unforeseen. On a less conscious
level there is the tendency, in the process of adapting to
painful reality, to pass from denial via exaggeration to a
justly proportioned estimate.[13] When, from inner or outer
pressures or both, the initial tendency to deny unpleasant
reality gives way, there is apt to be a breakthrough of nightmare fantasies. Only after the phase of exaggeration is a
realistic estimate achieved. To reject the alternatives of all
and none is thus a late and difficult achievement when it
comes to coping with realities which are exceedingly unpleasant. Exaggeration may not only supersede but also
continue denial, in an implicit feeling: it can't be as bad as
all that. And the next step of unconscious reasoning becomes:
nothing really terrible is going to happen.

While acknowledging the inadequacy of precedents as a
major source of prognostic error, let us consider what emotional factors may have contributed to specific mistaken
predictions. Take, for example, the overestimation of the
death rate and the inadequate anticipation of property destruction. The greater vulnerability of houses as compared
with people derives from the fact that while houses are
immobile people can take shelter. Since this seems almost
too obvious to mention, one must ask why the picture of
tremendous numbers of dead suggested itself rather than that
of destroyed homes of surviving people. As we shall see in
more detail later, disaster victims tend to lose interest in
during and for some time following the impact of
life itself. Persons instating themselves with active
in an anticipated disaster situation may react

in a similar way. Thus in their compassionate concern for those who would lose their lives, the forecasters may have felt relatively indifferent to merely material things. At the same time, an invitation to imagine extreme violence is apt to appeal also to latent sadistic impulses, which gain greater satisfaction from lurid prospects of gory death than from the less stimulating possibilities of property losses.

Of particular interest, I think, are the predictions of panic and madness. There was understandable gratification over the fact that these predictions proved quite false. There was no panic flight from London or any other city. Evacuation was orderly and fewer people than anticipated showed the wish to leave their homes for a safer location. One may suppose that in part reasonable government policies, of sharing information with the public, of leaving the possibility for evacuation always open, contributed to this result. However, was not the psychological readiness for panic overestimated? Among recent researchers on reactions to disaster it has become a commonplace that panic is the most often expected and least often occurring event in such situations.[14] Like most grossly mistaken predictions, the forecast of panic in disaster expresses an important fantasy. Reality, as is often the case, is poor in comparison with fantasy. Disaster-stricken populations, as we shall see more fully later, are apt to be quiet, stunned, and dazed. But in fantasy the idea of disaster evokes recurrently images like that in the film, *Quo Vadis,* where the desperate and shrieking populace of a Rome on fire flees like a wild herd through narrow passageways, bodies colliding and being trampled under foot, while each thinks only of saving himself. In the fantasy of panic there is the overpowering danger, the surge of the terrified and terrifying mob who have lost all regard for one another, the violent impact of bodies mutually entangled and trampling, the awful sense of disappearance of the benevolent and protective aspects of the world. Let us note here that such a scene makes a strong appeal to the imagination, which accounts for its being anticipated so much more often than it actually occurs. I shall attempt in the next part to suggest some of the underlying factors which may account for the fascination of this image, and I shall also undertake there to clarify the multiple meanings of the term "panic."

A further mistaken prediction of British experts before the last war was that there would be a tremendous outbreak of insanity. In the actual event no increase in mental disease was observed as compared with its peace-time incidence.[15] Behind the drastically mistaken prognosis we may discern certain fantasies evoked by the prospect of great danger. Damage to the mind may stand for physical mutilation which is frighteningly anticipated. Insanity is often feared in childhood and adolescence as a penalty for autoerotic activities. As the prospect of catastrophe is apt to be associated with the idea of punishment, the punishment of madness may also be drawn into the picture. Further, situations which combine temptation and punishment are particularly suited to rousing fears of insanity.[16] A threatening disaster represents a temptation to latent sadistic impulses, which can find vicarious satisfaction in it, while at the same time it carries the hazard of damage or destruction to the self. The terrible attraction of such a situation may rouse the feeling of being madly impelled to one's doom. The prospect of losing control over forbidden impulses also occasions fear of insanity. The expectation of participating directly or vicariously in destruction, of finding wicked gratification in scenes of carnage, evokes the idea of going mad.

The anticipated upsurge of insanity was apparently projected by the forecasters onto the masses of the people, to whom they implicitly attributed stronger impulses and weaker controls than their own. The forecasts of widespread madness and mass panic were probably closely related on an unconscious level. In both there would seem to be the fearful anticipation that the friendly human environment might undergo a nightmare transformation, with the lower impulses assuming the ascendancy. This apprehension may have been particularly pronounced in Britain, where reaction-formations against sadistic impulses seem typically to constitute major components of character.[17] Outer catastrophe is imagined as precipitating its counterpart in the subjective sphere: the destruction of defenses which make for gentleness and regard for others, and the unleashing of the dreaded sadistic drives.

There is another group of persons who occupy themselves with danger in a different way from those so far considered. These are the ones who choose professions in which the confrontation and mastery of danger play a central role—firemen, for example. Among the factors making for such a choice of occupation, we may note the "counter-phobic" defense.[18] Instead of avoiding a feared situation one may force oneself repeatedly to confront it as a proof that actually nothing terrible happens: one can face it and still survive. This applies to the daredevil, the man who drives a motorcycle through burning hoops, and so on, as well as to the one who faces danger in the role of a protector. Frequently the person who chooses an occupation in which protection and saving are prominent is reacting against earlier destructive impulses.

The person who becomes professionally occupied with warding off danger may be initially more fearful or more destructive than others, or may start from other motives. In any case, he is distinguished by the fact that he acquired a special set of skills for coping with danger. There are many occupations in which there is a more or less important component of facing dangerous or fearful things more than most people do. This confrontation of the fearful may or may not involve a risk. For the surgeon it does not; for the physician who treats contagious diseases it may. The policeman, the insurance agent, the undertaker confront in various ways dangers, risks, and fatalities. To round out our understanding of the manifold emotional resources for coping with danger it would be useful to study practitioners of such professions.

In addition to the range of individual attitudes towards possible disasters, there are general views of life and of the world, more or less elaborated, and varying from culture to culture, from group to group, as well as through time, which may include or exclude the prospect of catastrophe. Thus it was a traditional Jewish belief that the world would end with the terrible and comprehensive battle of Armageddon, which would usher in the millennium. There would have to be catastrophe and terror before paradise could be achieved. This was associated with the belief in a God who punished most those whom he most favored, and with, on an unconscious level, strong masochistic tendencies. Where such a belief about the world, about the relation of one's group to the powers that be, is strongly held, it may play a part in reactions to disaster when it comes. In the last war, according to some accounts, Eastern European Jews with strong religious beliefs were able to stand concentration camps better than those who had lost their faith.[20] If this is so, the inclusion of disaster in the long-term perspective may have had an effect of anticipatory inoculation, so that the individual was not completely taken by surprise. The belief in a God whose severe punishments did not imply a withdrawal of love from His chosen people may also have helped to make the sufferer feel not wholly abandoned. Similarly political beliefs which include the anticipation of violent conflicts may to some extent prepare those who hold them for disastrous experiences. So political prisoners in German concentration camps were less overwhelmed by their situation than non-political prisoners. What had happened to them was meaningful in terms of their antecedent scheme of life.[21] I shall have occasion to say more about factors such as these when I discuss reactions following a disaster, and the efforts to interpret what has happened in relation to the larger powers that rule the world.

3.
Denial of imminent threat

LET US NOW approach the situation where danger is imminent: in London during the last war when the air-raid sirens
sounded; in an American middle western town where there
has been a tornado warning and the storm starts blowing; or
where a river is rising towards flood tide; or in the life of a
single individual, when one faces an operation the next day.
These situations differ among themselves in the nature of
the threat involved, its degree of unexpectedness (a tornado,
for instance, being less expected than a bombing raid in war
time), its degree of uncertainty (one can doubt whether the
predicted tornado will materialize), its possible scope. However, all these threats have in common their temporal imminence, in contrast, for instance, to the threat of a possible
war with nuclear weapons in some indefinite future.

We have seen that in relation to remote threats the usual
reaction is one of being unworried, with the more or less
explicit belief that the threat will not materialize, or will
not affect oneself. This tendency to deny danger is likely to
carry over into situations of more imminent threat. Legends
of communal immunity may support the individual's belief
in his own insusceptibility to damage. In several towns where
tornado warnings went unheeded, it was recalled that an

Indian chief had told the early settlers that this location was proof against tornadoes because of a protecting hill or some other feature of the terrain.[22] It is perhaps significant that it should have been an Indian, representative of the dangers of the West to the early white settlers, who should have given the assurance of a protective environment. This old and mysterious wisdom may take precedence over the contemporary weather forecast through its congruence with the unconscious wish for magical protection.

However, in the main, the sense of immunity is sufficiently predominant that it requires little rationalization even in such simple terms. A threat, particularly of a danger not previously experienced, is simply not believed. A tornado victim in San Angelo, Texas, expresses her reactions to the warnings: "I hadn't been in one. . . . They warned us, but still I didn't think—well, it can't happen here."[23] A flood victim, speaking of the flood warnings which he heard over the radio, says: "I thought they were talking about the Kansas side. . . . I thought we were all right."[24] Another citizen of San Angelo, a printer, had heard about the tornado warning at the office of the newspaper for which he worked, but: "I didn't have any idea we would get to take part in that tornado." This sense of immunity is apt to persist until it is opposed by immediate sensory evidence. As it happened the printer and his wife were away from home when the tornado struck and destroyed their house. On their way home, they heard about the tornado and some of the damage it did, but immediately reassured themselves that the destroyed buildings were some distance from their home. As the wife puts it: "We had no idea we were included in it because we were further over. . . . You always believe it was the other guy, not yourself. We had no idea it included us."[25]

Here we have the feeling of personal immunity. Even when the denial of a threatened danger occurring (the initial belief that the tornado will not materialize) yields to contrary evidence, the belief remains: it can't affect me. The pre-disaster conviction seems to be: it can't happen, but if it does I will remain immune. As we shall see, there is a striking reversal of this view in the individual who actually undergoes a disaster (in the sense of direct impact): however widespread the damage, the first impression of the disaster victim is that he alone was hit.

Scepticism about sources of warnings follows from the need to deny the threatened danger, while ambivalence towards warning authorities serves further to justify the scepticism. A woman from San Angelo expresses this: "The day of the tornado my husband came in and told us that it had been on the radio . . . there was a tornado reported for San Angelo. And I said, 'Well, how do they know where a tornado is going to hit? Does anybody know?' I knew people were getting smarter. We're all supposed to be wiser, but still. . . . I just didn't think they knew anything about it."[26] Partly what seems to be expressed here is a sense of protest against anyone's being able to foretell catastrophe so surely. This sentiment is symbolized in the fate of the classical figure of Cassandra, whose dire predictions always aroused disbelief. Also the sources of warnings are authority figures who fall heir to a variety of mixed feelings going back to the relations of the child to his parents. Among other things, parents have the task of helping to initiate the child into the real world which is often frustrating and sometimes painful (visits to the doctor, for instance). The parents try to persuade the children that certain painful experiences are unavoidable, but the children often passionately doubt this. Such childhood feelings towards parents may carry over to authorities in adult life when they announce unwelcome events. There are probably considerable individual, as well as cultural, differences in reactions to the warnings of authorities, deriving from filial piety or rebelliousness, experience of more or less parental alarmism, and emphasis on being able to take hardship or on not being gullible.

Following a disaster further negative reactions towards sources of warning may appear. Thus one San Angelo tornado victim complained about the weather forecasters, saying that they were always scaring people with storm warnings.[27] It would seem that for him the authorities had become like worrisome parents who plague the child with their apprehensions of constant dangers. Another citizen of San Angelo had the opposite complaint: that the radio did not give enough storm warnings. At the time when the tornado hit, she had turned off her radio because of too much static and so had not heard the tornado alarm.[28] Thus she had been taken by surprise (though many who heard the warning were equally taken by surprise because they discounted it). She apparently blamed the authorities for not preparing her better, in a similar spirit to that of the child who feels his parents have kept things from him and left him to face painful experiences unprepared.

I have spoken before of the tendency to associate disastrous experiences from whatever source with punishment. In keeping with this, warnings of danger may be felt as threats of punishment. To some Londoners during the Blitz the shrieking sirens sounded like the accusing and menacing screams of an angry mother.[29]

As to the feeling of immunity, it may be, paradoxically, especially strong when there is nothing one can do to ward off an impending danger. If there is something one can do as a precaution, one may acknowledge the threat to the extent of taking the precautionary measures at one's disposal. Where there is nothing one can do, denial of the threat continues to recommend itself as a defense against anxiety. The woman from San Angelo who doubted the tornado warnings, saying that she didn't think anyone was smart enough to know that, went on to acknowledge: "We didn't have any place to go and didn't know which direction to run ... I couldn't have gone anywhere for protection. ... No one around us had a cellar. ... No one had ever said they had a cellar and invited us to come to it in case a tornado or something was to happen."[30] As there was no precautionary action which she could take, she mustered all the scepticism she could about the warnings.

An illustration of this type of reaction from the political sphere may be found in the attitudes of French politicians at the present time to the prospect of a future war. Since they feel that France lacks the capacity to deter, or to cope with, such an eventuality, they avoid considering what the shape and cost of another war might be. The degree of this avoidance is greater than in Britain or America.[31]

Where acknowledging a threat would involve considerable inconvenience (in the troublesome precautions which would then be indicated) the tendency to deny the danger is further reenforced. This appears in people's unwillingness to evacuate their homes when threatened with floods or hurricanes. The certain inconvenience of evacuation outweighs the greater, but less certain, hazard of being overtaken by the disaster. The reaction is similar to that of the person who puts off a visit to the dentist. The prospect of immediate pain arouses more distress than the more remote possibility of losing his teeth, which tends to seem rather unreal. The unwillingness to take the steps necessary to avoid a catastrophe thus strengthens the tendency to deny that it can happen. Also where, in a threatened flood or hurricane, evacuation is called for, people may be concerned about their property, which they wish to stay and guard, while they do not consider the possibility of any threat of life.[32] As we shall see later, this attitude becomes reversed following the impact of disaster. When a threat to life has actually materialized, there is apt to be a drastic reduction of concern about property.

There are perhaps certain aspects of American culture which contribute to the tendency to deny possible on-coming disaster. One of these is a strong repudiation of anxious, worrisome or fearful tendencies. Children are taught from an early age not to be "scaredy-cats." The "over-protective" mother who hovers apprehensively over her child is a very negative figure from the American point of view. This contrasts with certain other cultures, for instance the Eastern European Jewish[33] or the pre-Soviet Russian,[34] in which incessant maternal anxiety about threats to health and the fragility of life pervaded the family atmosphere. For Americans, such anxiousness is not only futile and unnecessary, it is incompatible with a positive image of oneself. It is essential to one's self-esteem to feel: everything is OK with me. We shall see later what an important role this plays in post-disaster reactions, in which a major theme is: "we were lucky" —in spite of everything that happened. In American culture, emotional effusion, particularly of distressed feelings, is negative; doing something useful is positive. The American feeling about anxiety seems to be that it should be strictly confined to a signal function, to set off effective action. Thus there is "no use" in worrying if there is nothing you can do. We have seen that this was explicitly a major attitude about a remote threat like that of nuclear warfare: "There's nothing a person can do, so what's the use of worrying?" If there is something one can do, in a more immediate danger situation, then one should proceed to do it with a minimum of upset.

If one is impressed by a threatened danger and becomes alarmed about it, it begins to loom large and one begins to feel oneself becoming small. One acknowledges the sway of superior powers and feels again like a child. In America, where reverting to childhood, in the sense of becoming again dependent, is very negative,[35] and where, on the other hand, being big and tough and not easily overawed are positive, the tendency to deny a threatening danger is further reenforced. If one laughs it off, the hazard seems small and one can continue to feel big oneself.

The negative evaluation of worry about possible future hazards was expressed by one of the exceptional tornado victims (among those interviewed) who had taken advance warnings at all seriously. Several days before the event, he had read a tornado forecast in the newspaper and had discussed with his wife how you could tell if one was coming and what she and the children should do if a tornado hit while he was away from home. As it turned out this forethought was quite reasonable and useful. Yet in telling about it afterwards, the young man stresses that it was "just casual conversation, see? Regular breakfast table conversation."[36] Rather than feeling proud of his preparedness, he is concerned with warding off the suspicion that he might have been fussy and worrisome. To a certain extent preparing in advance for such contingencies may also be felt as an admission of weakness: one should be able to cope with things on the spot, if one is really strong and resourceful, without cautious rehearsals ahead of time.

The value of keeping calm, both as an end in itself and as a condition for effective activity, is often stressed by American disaster victims. We shall see instances of it in the impact phase and following. It is equally important in moments of anticipation. Thus a woman from San Angelo tells how she discussed the tornado warning with her next-door neighbor: "So I asked her what we should do if we did have one, because we didn't have a storm cellar at that time. . . . She said, well, she thought the main thing was to be calm. And I thought that was a very good suggestion. . . . The lady next-door here, she is a very calm person and I felt a whole lot better after I talked to her."[37] One gets the impression here that a calm feeling is as good as a storm cellar. It would seem that what is feared is excitement more than physical danger. At the same time if one does not get excited, probably the belief that anything bad will happen is weakened. On the basis of unconscious beliefs about connections between inner and outer events, one may feel that inner turmoil is a portent of storm. Such a connection is often expressed in movies, for instance, where at a climactic moment in the lives of the protagonists the sky darkens, there is a rumbling of thunder, and a storm breaks out.

Control of apprehensive feelings must also be maintained by grown-ups as an example to children. Another woman in San Angelo says that since the tornado some parents too readily run to school to bring their children home when a storm blows up. She herself tries to keep such activity to a minimum, because: "Fear must not control you, and you must not run every time you get scared." Another mother from the same town says about her children: "We don't want them to go through life frightened of every little cloud that comes up."[38]

With denial and low anxiety there is little inclination to conjure up fantasies of disaster. One does not believe it until one sees it. So, for instance, in Kansas, in the face of a predicted and oncoming flood, people were inclined to say: "We'll wait and see what happens."[39] The rising river and the repeated flood warnings did not seem to stimulate any vivid images of the river overwhelming the town. Refusal to picture this possibility was of course supported by the fact that to acknowledge the danger would entail the inconvenience of evacuation. Also people may have felt that it would have been rather weak and discreditable, a "scaredy-cat" reaction, to take flight from a danger which had not yet fully materialized and might recede instead of advancing further.

Americans seem little inclined to "avalanche" fantasies, that is, to imagining that once something threatening gets started, even on a small scale, there is no telling where it will end. So, again in Kansas, the reaction to the rising water was at each moment: "It can't go any higher."[40]

Even where the past provides a precedent for disaster (if it was not in one's own recent past experience), there is a tendency to deny that this is any portent for the future. One expects things to be better now than in the bad old days. The recent flood victims in Kansas knew about earlier floods in their area, but did not believe in the possibility of recurrence because dikes had been raised in the meantime. As one of them said: "My folks went through the 1903 flood. . . . But we had dikes this time. I wasn't worried."[41]

Who are those who acknowledge imminent dangers which others deny? If we take the man from Arkansas already mentioned, who took the newspaper prediction of tornadoes sufficiently seriously to discuss with his wife in detail what they should do in such an event, we find that he emphasizes repeatedly that throughout the subsequent happenings he did not get excited or upset or lose his emotional control. He appeared to be more than usually concerned with the danger of emotional disturbance.[42] One might advance the hypothesis that one condition for taking warnings of imminent danger seriously would be fear of loss of emotional control (in whatever form the individual imagines this) which might be precipitated by an unforeseen situation. Formulating in advance the steps to be taken in this or that contingency provides a safeguard against the eruption of unpremeditated feelings and impulses.

While most of the disaster victims interviewed emphasized the unexpectedness of the experience, a few claimed to have had presentiments, and this quite apart from broadcast or published warnings. In the material I have seen these were aging women. A fifty-four-year-old widow in Arkansas tells of having watched the darkening storm clouds and says: "I think it turned out just like I felt it—like it was going to that evening—because I never had such a feeling in all my life. That is the reason I kept telling my son—my little—my son to get prepared for it, that I really felt it in my bones, somehow, I just felt it, you know. I don't know why people have those feelings, but somehow or another I just felt like it was going to be destroyed there, that very evening."[43] An elderly woman from San Angelo tells of leaving her son's house for the last time before it was destroyed by the tornado: "And when I walked off that porch and walked to the car, something just told me so plain. I just kinda looked back, and when I looked back, well, something just told me, like you would be sitting there, 'You won't never go in that house no more.' And I didn't."[44]

We may readily suppose that these "presentiments" are constructed in retrospect out of indefinite feelings of depression, loss, and apprehensiveness (to which some aging women are particularly subject), which at other times may lack specific content, but which on this occasion could be given meaning by the catastrophe which followed. A certain gloomy triumph may thus be achieved in finding a justification for one's low spirits and in feeling wiser (rather than less lucky) than more carefree people.

I should like now to consider the consequences of denial of danger which persists up to the point when the disaster occurs. There is likely to be more emotional disturbance following the event on the part of those who beforehand warded off all anxiety, and denied the reality of the threat, than on the part of those who were able to tolerate some anticipatory alarm and to acknowledge that the disaster could happen. Anticipation constitutes a small-scale preliminary exposure on the level of imagination and can have an inoculating effect. By rehearsing and familiarizing oneself with the coming event one may reduce the risk of being overwhelmed by the experience.

I have the impression that among tornado victims who have been studied those who denied the danger in advance had the more intense fears of a repetition of the catastrophe afterwards, and became more acutely sensitive to every warning sign. In this we may see a need to master the trauma of a sudden overpowering experience by repeating it in imagination. It also seems that these individuals show, as it were, a tardy obedience to the imagined warning and punishing powers who are felt to have inflicted the disaster. It is as if they say: I have learned my lesson; I am chastened; I will not take your warnings lightly another time; I know now that you mean it, and how hard you can hit.

Observations on soldiers and citizens in war time similarly suggest that anticipatory denial predisposes to subsequent disturbances. Among air force personnel, those who were most unrealistically enthusiastic about combat beforehand were more likely than others to lose their sense of invulnerability in actual danger situations and to show subsequent neurotic disturbances.[45] It has been suggested by Irving Janis that a qualified rather than a total belief in immunity constitutes a favorable condition for withstanding extreme events.[46] The individual who to retain his sense of safety must deny that anything terrible will happen has his feeling of security shattered when danger materializes. The person who admits that extremely dangerous events may occur, but retains the belief that he himself will survive, is the one who is apt to emerge from danger with less disturbance. In some situations, as for instance for a member of a bomber crew, both anticipations contain elements of improbability: whether one assumes that no damage can occur to the plane, or whether one supposes that the plane may be hit but that nevertheless one will escape damage oneself. If the latter anticipation is prognostic of better tolerance for stress than the former, it may be for this reason. The person who acknowledges the possibility of danger hitting very close to him may have the confidence that he can take it. The one who, on the other hand, has to imagine an area of safety always surrounding himself has the implicit feeling that he cannot take it if a real hazard comes too close. Similarly with physical injuries, there are individuals who have an all-or-none attitude: anything less than complete physical intactness is devastating for them. Others are able to react in a more differentiated way to various degrees of damage.

Denial of danger and avoidance of anxiety become the more difficult to maintain in the face of imminent danger acknowledged by those around one, as in the course of bombing raids in war time. Here continued denial may be related to peculiarly terrifying repressed fantasies of what the threatened danger might be. The attempt to avoid anxiety may express the fear of immediate and uncontrollable transition from the slightest apprehensiveness to overwhelming and intolerable dread. In fact, where persons exposed to wartime bombing denied feeling any fear or anxiety, this was sometimes followed by neurotic or psychotic breakdown.[47] Thus either the reality stimuli broke through, undoing the denial and precipitating the dreaded emotions, or the denial had to be reenforced in a more drastic departure from reality.

Accurate information about what to expect may not only mitigate painful reactions in the danger situation but also reduce the tendency towards denial beforehand. One of the motives of denial derives from nightmarish fantasies about what may happen, which one tries to exclude from consciousness because they are too frightening. If a more realistic prognosis is less terrible than these fantasies, it may facilitate facing the danger.[48] But we should also note that the reality to be anticipated may be worse than the fantasies about it. In this case precise information is not likely to reduce anxiety or to increase readiness to acknowledge the danger ahead.

I should like to bring together now the hypotheses arrived at so far about the relation of denial to different time phases of a disaster. First, however, it may be well to clarify the meaning of "denial." The term "denial" as I use it here covers a range of phenomena: (a) Low cathexis, that is, slight or rare concern with an unpleasant fact or prospect, which is mainly disregarded. (b) Repression, that is, an effortful exclusion from consciousness of a painful idea, which is sometimes combined with a conscious belief which negates it. (c) Isolation of affect, that is, disassociation from an idea (which remains conscious) of the emotion related to it, as in a merely verbal acceptance. (d) An intellectual and emotional acknowledgment of an unpleasant reality where the individual continues nevertheless to behave as if it were not so.

In all these cases there is this in common: that the individual does not react fully to a danger, future, present, or past. What I wish to bring out is that denial of danger is in certain moments neither pathological (symptomatic of emotional disturbance) nor pathogenic (productive of emotional disturbance). It is a question of discriminating under what circumstances this is a benevolent defense and when it is the reverse.

In the case of a remote threat, we have seen that denial seems to be the usual reaction, except where emotional disturbances (such as fear of eruption of intense hostile impulses) find an external counterpart in prospects of catastrophe. Fear of remote threats thus appears to be pathological in the sense that it is symptomatic of emotional disturbances. At the same time the individual who attaches distress from other sources to the idea of a coming disaster may incorporate more or less reality into the picture. He may become a prophet of the end of the world, or he may make a careful study of the weapons of contemporary warfare. In the latter case motives of private distress may attain public usefulness. As to the tendency towards denial of remote threats, I think that it can be called "normal" in the sense that it is indicative of a relatively low level of emotional disturbance. Exceptions to this occur in neurotics whose worries attach to other prospects, who repress their anxieties, who take a counter-phobic attitude towards danger, or whose withdrawal from reality makes them impervious to it. In other words, the "normal" person is not apt to worry about remote threats, though not everyone who is free from such worry is "normal."

When it comes to more immediate threats denial appears in a different light. It is necessary, of course, to distinguish here degrees of uncertainty of an oncoming danger. We may say that the more predictable the danger, the more patho-logical the denial. However, in any case where denial is main-tained in an immediate pre-disaster situation, we may advance the hypothesis that it is pathogenic (whether pathological or not), that is, that it is more conducive to subsequent disturb-ance than some degree of anticipatory acknowledgment of the threat. The lack of emotional preparation, the sudden shattering of the fantasy of complete immunity, the sense of compunction for failing to respond to warnings contribute to the disruptive effect of an extreme event the possibility of which has been denied up to the last moment.

4.
Precautions and propitiation

\Λ\ΛΛΛΛΛΛΛΛΛΛΛΛΛΛΛΛΛΛΛΛΛΛΛΛΛ\
.V.V.V.V.V.V.V.V.V.V.V.V.V.V.V.V.V.V.V.V.V.V.V.V\

LET US TURN now to the situation where a threat is admitted, an oncoming danger is acknowledged. This may be where a disaster has already occurred (the anticipation of future tornadoes on the part of a tornado-stricken community), or in a situation of continuous intermittent danger, as of soldiers in war time, or the inhabitants of a city subject to bombing. Where a coming danger is thus anticipated there are generally certain precautionary measures prepared in advance and put into effect when the danger is at hand. People's feelings about such precautionary measures are not exclusively determined by their realistic protective potential. Sometimes one feels unconsciously that resort to a protective device will magically prevent the threatening danger. Do we not often say: when I take my umbrella it never rains? In a similar way in Britain during the Blitz it was observed that some people had the conviction that when they carried their gas masks there would not be a raid.[49] Going to a storm shelter may be felt in the same way, not as a protection against a tornado but as an insurance that none will occur. This expectation would seem to have been present in a woman from Arkansas who with her family successfully weathered a tornado in a storm house to which she had had recourse many times before when it had been a false alarm. This time, after the tornado had really hit and destroyed her house, even though the storm house had been a life-saver, she was filled with doubts about the future usefulness of the shelter. She became preoccupied with thoughts of what might have happened, and considered that the storm house had only stood up through luck because it was not in the direct path of the tornado.[50] While it may have been the case that this woman's storm house had deficiencies of which she only became aware after disaster struck, it also seems likely that her disillusionment with her shelter related to the previous implicit, now disproved belief that going to the shelter would prevent the occurrence of a disastrous storm.

Rules of safety, as we have already observed, are often unconsciously equated with rules of obedience. Sometimes people's observance of safety measures shows directly that they are reacting more to the enforcing authorities than to the real danger. So in Britain during the Blitz it was observed that some people were more careful to black out their front windows than their back ones. Evidently to the bombers overhead it made no difference whether a gleam of light shone from the back or the front of the house. Being less careful about the back windows could only mean that one expected less supervision of the wardens at the backs of houses, one ran less risk of rebuke by the authorities.[51]

Rebellion against authorities may lead to outspoken refusal of the precautions they have imposed. Thus a woman from Texas expresses her repudiation of the storm cellar to which her mother used to drag her against her will when she was a child: "I wouldn't go to a storm house if I had one out there. My mother dragged me in one all my life. I said then if I ever got away I wouldn't go any more. . . She always dragged us to the storm house, and I said I never knew it to do any good. We always had to go back through the rain and the mud, and we always lost a lot of sleep, and I never could see any use. . . I never shall forget going to the storm house one time when it was covered over with logs ... and I looked up and saw a great big snake up over us, you know. . . And I was even afraid to say anything about it . . . but it frightened me to lie there and look at the thing."[52] Here is an expression of the child's sense of vehement protest against precautionary measures which involve fear and discomfort in themselves, which the mother imposes with the assurance that they are necessary to ward off greater dangers, but where the child does not believe this. The child, now grown up, fulfills her earlier resolve not to do any more what mother used to make her do, to emancipate herself from mother's precautionary routines.

In observing prescribed precautions one may feel unconsciously that one is being good in a moral sense, and may exempt oneself from continued observance when one feels one has built up a sufficient score of goodness. This is similar to the way in which the child who has been good for some time feels that he is entitled to cut loose a bit and that his parents will not view it too severely, or the kind of compromises that we all make with our consciences. Again in wartime Britain, the story was told of three sisters who went to the public shelters every night with the exception of Saturday, when they permitted themselves the luxury of sleeping at home. One Saturday night all three were killed by a bomb. Evidently the intermission they permitted themselves was unrelated to the utility of the safety rules. But they apparently felt that having been so good all week they were entitled to a little pleasure in recompense.[53]

Ideally one should behave according to the realistic efficacy of various precautionary measures apart from the emotions evoked by the authorities who inculcate them. In practice, however, it is often difficult to make an assessment of efficacy with any high degree of confidence. Thus faith in the authorities or distrust of them, inclinations towards compliance or rebellion, are apt to sway the balance. Compliance may produce a gratified sense of goodness or distress at having given in again like an intimidated child. In everyday life, do not many people feel a certain chagrin about wearing rubbers? One is unsure how indispensable it is to health, but one remembers very well how mother used to nag about it.

Attitudes towards precautions may also be affected by emotional connotations specific to particular protective devices. The strangeness of the situation into which one is forced for purposes of security, combined with the emotionally fraught presence of danger, may evoke a variety of latent tendencies. The requirement of remaining for a considerable time underground, the unusual proximity of strangers, or the necessity of staying in the dark may rouse in some persons intense anxiety. For the individual with claustrophobic susceptibilities, for instance, any danger in the open may be preferable to the terrors of an inclosed place of refuge. Others may have adequate defenses for accommodating themselves to such circumstances, while still others may find them gratifying. Thus for some people the opportunity for increased social contact provided by a communal shelter may be rewarding in itself.[54] On the basis of such factors various precautionary measures may be preferred or shunned quite apart from their protective efficacy.

Insofar as an imminent danger is felt as a threat of punishment for bad behavior, various propitiatory manoeuvers may be undertaken with the aim of dissuading the punishing authorities. Here again the rationale is often unconscious and the procedure disguised. In *Myths of War*, Marie Bonaparte analyzes propitiatory devices of this sort. During the last war there was a widespread belief among French soldiers that something was put in their wine ration which reduced sexual desire and potency (and of course similar rumors have been current in other armies). In other times and places, a part of the ritual observed by warriors in preparation for going into battle was a period of abstention from sexual intercourse. According to the unconscious logic, the imminent threat to body intactness and to life itself was construed as punishment for sexual activity. Renunciation of sex was thus undertaken as a means of propitiating the threatening powers and of warding off the feared punishment. In contemporary life, where conscious belief in the efficacy of

renunciatory and other rituals to placate the gods and win
their protection has waned, one finds more indirect expression of the same motives, as in the myth of the doctored
wine. Here soldiers from unconscious fear of punishment
experience a reduction of their sexual desires and capacities,
which, on the conscious level, is unintelligible to them. They
then blame the authorities, external counterparts of their
own threatening conscience, for having imposed an unwelcome restriction.[55] According to some observers, Londoners
during the early phase of the Blitz manifested a tendency
towards increased asceticism, presumably from similar unconscious propitiatory motives.[56]

Any upsurge of impulses which arouse guilt and are felt
as likely to incur retribution may increase the individual's
alarm in a danger situation where he feels he must be good
and placating. The intensification of aggressive impulses
which some patients feel on the eve of an operation com-
plicates their emotional predicament in this way. They feel
that they must control their hostility so as not to antagonize
their environment and they tend to project their negative
feelings so that the environment appears increasingly threatening.[57]

An opposite reaction to that of propitiatory renunciation
is that of orgiastic indulgence in times of extreme danger.
If tomorrow we may die, we might as well eat, drink and
be merry today. The mechanisms involved in such a reaction
are probably various and complicated. There is a sense of
there being little time left to enjoy all that one would wish.
One may want to make up for missed opportunities of the
past, renounced in the hope of a later reward which now
becomes highly dubious. There may be the feeling that since
I stand a good chance to pay the penalty, I may as well have
something in exchange. The conception of the powers that
govern one's fate is undoubtedly a different one than in the
case of attempted propitiation. For those who find sanction
for increased gratification in a time of danger, it would seem
that the justice of the powers has become subject to doubt.
The powers seem capricious, equally ready to punish the

virtuous and the wicked, so what is the point of being good? Also, if such disastrous things can happen, are not the powers themselves wicked? The reaction is like that of a child who becomes naughty when he has had some revelation which destroys his belief in the ideal character of his parents. The effort to be good is predicated on the existence of good parent-figures. If they on their side are not good, the contract is vitiated. Or perhaps if so many evil things happen the gods do not exist at all; or, as Epicurus thought, even if they exist, they take no interest in human affairs. It is then mistaken and futile to try to obtain indulgence or protection by sacrifice of pleasure.

Among the complicated and conflicting feelings about sex there is not only that of its exposing one to punishment but also that of insuring one against death or fear of death in the sense of triumphant vitality, in the promise of immortality through procreation, sometimes expressed in the mystical belief in love conquering death. An imminent danger situation may thus stimulate increased sexual intensity in some individuals, with the implicit feeling that procreation wards off the danger of death.[58] The impatient longing of many young soldiers to beget a child may express this wish to immortalize themselves, as well as the wish to fill out the phases of life which are their due in what may be a very limited time. The personages of Boccaccio's *Decameron,* having taken refuge from a plague-stricken city, occupied themselves with tales of triumphant sexual license. In London during the great plague of 1665, increased sexual liberty was said to have flourished, helped on by the rumor that venereal disease immunized one to the more dreaded disease.[59] Here there may have been the implicit assertion that the punishment for sex is specific to it (it does not expose one to every fatality), as well as the idea of paying by a lesser evil for exemption from a greater one.

The question arises under what circumstances and for which individuals a persisting threat evokes propitiatory renunciation and when and for whom there is a tendency rather to orgiastic emancipation. It has been suggested that where there is a high degree of threat which continues regardless of what the individual does there is apt to be an increase in impulsive freedom.[60] However, this leaves out of account what the individual may feel that he can do on a supernatural as well as a natural level, for instance in propitiatory observances. One might say that uncertainty as to one's fate is a precondition of propitiatory behavior. If the outcome is certain, abandonment to the gratification of impulses might be more likely. In a recent French play, *N'Importe Quoi Pour Elle*, a woman who has been condemned to death as a political offender spends her remaining days continuously in the arms of her lover. The conjuring up in fantasy of such a situation has in part a liberating effect in dispensing with the worries related to an uncertain future and the anxiety that what one does may influence one's fate adversely. At the same time, in the imagined situation, the sense of heightened life in all-absorbing sexual pleasure helps to ward off the fear of death.

Belief or disbelief in life after death may also make a decisive difference. If one believes in an after-life in which one's fate may be better or worse depending on one's conduct in this life, then propitiatory goodness has a meaning even if one is under sentence of death. But also where there is no belief in an after-life, anticipation of death may be far from producing emancipation for the pursuit of pleasure. Rather we might expect it to cause depression and incapacity for enjoyment. In such a reaction the individual's conscience confirms the judgment which he feels has fallen upon him.

I would think that in any danger situation where the outcome is less than certain the inclination towards propitiatory behavior or the opposite would be largely determined by the individual's beliefs and fantasies about the powers that rule the world and his relation to them. These ideas derive from early experiences with the powers who presided over the child's life, meting out rewards and punishments justly or capriciously, namely, the parents, as well as beliefs derived from religious teachings, and folklore about luck and fate. The main factors which affect propitiatory or orgiastic reactions in a situation of anticipated danger would seem to be: the certainty or uncertainty of the outcome, beliefs about one's ability to influence it, and compliance or rebellion towards punishing powers. I shall come back to this subject later when I discuss reactions following an accomplished disaster, and the various ways in which it is interpreted.

5.
Experience and expectations

∿∿∿∿∿∿∿∿∿∿∿∿∿∿∿∿∿∿∿∿

ANTICIPATIONS of danger may be affected in a number of ways by the fact of having undergone a disastrous experience. As we shall see in more detail later, a frequent reaction to a disaster is the anxious expectation of an imminent repetition of the event. This attitude, while manifestly forward-looking, may be in effect directed more towards the emotional mastery of the past trauma. Brooding about what to do if it should happen again involves reliving the recently experienced catastrophe until one may be able to recall it without unbearable distress. Where emotional tolerance for the past experience is the main aim of such thinking, the problem of precautions against future dangers may fade out as the traumatic effect wears off.

Sometimes following a disaster previous habits of denial of danger become reestablished in what seems to be very slightly modified form. As one woman from San Angelo put it: "We don't have a storm cellar and of course we don't watch clouds here on that account. Because of course if we don't watch them we don't know how bad it's going to be."[61] This is the same woman who said that before the tornado she had disbelieved the warnings and that anyhow there was nothing she could have done because they had no storm cellar. Following the event we see the same mutually involved denial tendencies and lack of means of protection. However, one may perhaps see a difference in emphasis in the post-disaster attitude in that there is more conscious effort to avoid becoming aware of danger signals. Denial has become more difficult, less automatic, more a matter of policy. Intentional avoidance of alarming stimuli is observed as a defense against anxiety, and even as a magical means of warding off the external threat. It is not only that this woman does not want to know about impending danger but that she feels if one does not react it ceases to exist. Thus she says: "If you watch the cloud then naturally you're afraid it's going to hit. But if you don't watch the cloud, well, you see, then everything will be all right. You just control your mind." And, implicitly, by controlling your mind you control reality. (This woman is unlike most of her neighbors, who following the tornado prepared in various ways for possible recurrence. The persistence of the pre-disaster routine in this case seems to be related to an eccentric family pattern: the woman described her husband as "peculiar" and says that in general he is unwilling to make any adaptation to changing times. Thus, for instance, when the children ask to have a telephone installed, he refuses, saying there was none in the house in which he was brought up.)

Refusal to change in response to an increasingly threatening danger and where extreme events have already occurred is a method of maintaining denial of the threat. Thus in Britain, in the early days of the bombing of London, people in unaffected towns were at first very reluctant to take evacuees into their homes. They resisted making any change in their accustomed routine of life, since such changes would represent an acknowledgment of the danger situation. Not speaking about what has happened serves a similar defensive function. So in some of the unbombed cities in England it was practically taboo to speak of the events occurring in London and other cities which suffered bombing raids. By being excluded from conversation these painful events were excluded from reality. If they entered one's safe little world even in conversation it might be that they could break in totally.[62]

These devices of not noticing, not speaking about, not making any changes in deference to, a threatening danger, all have the significance of magically controlling or abolishing it. Evidently the occurrence of disaster may stimulate efforts of control of a more realistic sort, although these too may be unconsciously invested with exaggerated power.

In contrast to those who ward off awareness of danger signals, people who have been exposed to an extreme event may become intensely alert to indicators of its recurrence. This watchfulness may have the purpose of protecting one from being taken again by surprise. Thus a tornado victim speaking of the past event, in which she had discounted warning signs, and her present attitude of foresight and alertness, says: "I figured it was just a lot of wind with some hail in it. It never entered my mind anything about a tornado. Well, I watch the clouds a little closer now. I'm not going to let them slip up on me like that."[63] Another woman who had undergone the same experience speaks of having gained confidence through watchfulness and knowledge in being able to tell in advance what will happen: "If I see a cloud coming up I go out and look at it and then I can pretty well tell what it's going to do. You can kind of study those things and discover what they're going to do. You can tell."[64] Similarly a young man from the same area tells of how, when a recent storm was coming up, he ran out of the house to look at the ominous cloud, and, as a fence blocked his view of the horizon, climbed the fence to get a fuller view. He remarks that he was not in the least frightened: "I was watching it. I was trying to keep my eyes open and watch it and see as much as possible to see what was going to happen. In fact that's why she (his wife) got kind of aggravated with me for taking so long watching it on the fence. She wanted to get going (to get in the car and drive away from the storm), and I wanted to watch it a little more to see what it was going to develop into."[65]

While such alertness and acquired knowledge of prognostic signs may certainly be useful, it may also be unconsciously overestimated. There may be the feeling that an object you keep your eye on cannot harm you; there are many beliefs about the immobilizing power of the eye. One is apt to feel not helpless or passive, but in control of that which one knows. What one knows all about may seem domesticated and diminished by being known. Or one may feel that in predicting one makes the thing happen: there is an elating sense of power in having made a correct prediction. Thus there may be a component of fantasied magic control in keeping one's eye on the danger source just as in refusing to recognize it, though the alert individual evidently assimilates more of reality. We know little about what it is that disposes some individuals to prefer keeping their eyes closed and others to prefer keeping their eyes open to a threatening danger, a question which falls under the general heading of choice of defense mechanisms.

Rehearsal in imagination or in actuality of what one would do in an emergency may also serve to reduce anticipatory anxiety. One pictures oneself in action rather than overwhelmed by distress. The image of oneself as a rescuer pushes aside that of one's being a victim. The mother of a fifteen-year-old boy, whose scout troop prepares for action in emergencies, tells how her son anticipates a possible recurrence of the tornado they have experienced: "He says, 'I don't feel like I want to get panicky or go running around or nothing like that . . . What I want to do is just watch, and try and stay in contact with the radio station . . . to stay in communication with the proper authorities. And,' he says, 'try to hold myself in readiness where something was to happen, then I could do what was expected of me.' "[66] Here the requirements of alertness and useful activity are explicitly put forward as excluding panicky feelings and uncoordinated movements. For this young boy, moreover, authorities who will tell him what to do constitute a safeguard against being emotionally overwhelmed. Confidence in know-how, with the image of oneself as doing skillful and useful things, strengthens the feeling one can remain in control in a danger situation.

Everyday life abounds in dangers, such as those of traffic for both autoists and pedestrians, to which one does not react with any feeling of alarm; one is only slightly aware of them, and one has confidence in one's habits of precaution. When a new hazard has been added and new precautionary measures have after some time become habitual, this also tends to become assimilated into the usual background of life. Emotional reaction to the hazard becomes slight. One knows what one can do about it, and one even at times omits taking the indicated precautions (just as one may exceed the speed limit) with a certain nonchalance. So in London after the Blitz had been going on for some time, people began to take it in the same way as one does traffic hazards.[67] In a similar spirit a woman from San Angelo speaks of the habit of life which has come to include going to storm cellars in the year following the disastrous tornado: "We have a big cellar . . . In fact we have as many as twenty-seven in there at one time . . . All the neighbors go to the cellars nowadays out here . . . But when we're down there we just talk and laugh. We have a club meeting down there . . . The kiddos named it our 'Tornado Club.' "[68]

6.
Danger shared

WHERE DANGER THREATENS a large number of people at once
one is apt to feel differently about it than one does when
facing danger alone (as in an operation, for example). We
shall see, in the phase of impact of a large-scale disaster and
following it, many ways in which reactions are affected by
the communal character of the experience. In the anticipatory phase, when a danger source may as yet have made only
an exciting break with everyday routine and people still
doubt that any serious damage will be done, a holiday atmosphere sometimes prevails. So, for instance, on the eve of a
flood of the Rio Grande, as torrents of the swollen river
rushed and seethed, people in festive mood crowded the river
banks and the bridge to watch the "Bravo" acting up.[69]
Instead of engaging in precautionary activity, such as remov-
ing their belongings to high ground, people here regarded
the danger source as a fine spectacle. In a similar way, in the
beginning hours of the great Chicago fire, people in the better part of town, across the river from where the fire started,
unsuspecting as yet that it could touch them, gathered in a
gay, excited mood to watch the tremendous sight.[70] The
pleasure in the spectacle of a great force unleashed may come
partly from a feeling of identification with, or participation

(45)

in it. The enjoyment of such a sight may also derive in part from a sense of mastery over earlier, childhood fears—the fear of the little child who runs back in alarm from the roar and leap of the oncoming wave on the beach, or who is frightened of the fire. Being able to face once frightening stimuli produces a feeling of elation; the excitement evoked takes on a positive quality. Such mastery over earlier fright is achieved from experiences in which the feared danger did not materialize—one was able to swim up through the wave instead of being overwhelmed; the fire remained safely within bounds. The sense of confidence thus established becomes deceptive if applied to the same elements at times when they are eluding control.

The enjoyment of the spectacle, rather than alarm about the danger, is facilitated by the presence of others. The lonely spectator of a roaring torrent might feel uneasy; the spectator surrounded by a good-humored crowd feels protected. Even where the threat is more acknowledged, as in anticipation of a bombing raid, being surrounded by people who are calm and confident has a marked effect of reducing anxiety. Just as for the young child the cue to danger was most often provided by his parents' alarm and the indication of safety by their equanimity, so in later situations the responses of others give one the signal for how to take it. This applies also to a change in evalution of an imminent threat. Where physical signs and broadcast warnings may have left people unaffected, they may begin to be alarmed where they see others taking the potential danger seriously. So, for instance, on the occasion of an oncoming flood, one person says: "I heard the whistles blow (the signal to evacuate), but nobody left so I didn't either." Another in the same situation states: "I didn't believe it (when she heard the flood warnings). Then I saw other people leaving and I got scared."[71]

Alarm about an impending danger may be aroused or intensified by other people's expressions of fear or gloomy forecasts. According to some writers, however, being in a group more often has the effect of reducing anxiety.[72] One of the earliest childhood fears is that of being abandoned, and, as I shall try to show later, one of the most traumatic effects of disaster comes from the temporary feeling of having been wholly forsaken. The presence of others in moments of anticipated danger reduces the dread of abandonment. Since in early life it was the parents' calm which quieted the child's fears (when he awoke from a nightmare, for example), so in a situation where some are frightened and others confident, it is apt to be the latter who gain the greater influence, inheriting the role of strong parent-figures. If a threat is sufficiently serious to rouse common anxiety, the individual may at least gain some comfort from the realization that he is not the only one who is afraid.

Sometimes, as we have seen, the presence of others, because of its reassuring effects, reenforces the tendency to deny an imminent danger. At other times, being with others may facilitate a correct estimate of the danger situation. The latter effect has been observed where it is a question of interpreting ambiguous cues of an oncoming event. So, for instance, with the sound of an approaching tornado, persons who were alone when they heard it more often interpreted it as the noise of a train or some other ordinary and non-alarming event. Those who, on the other hand, discussed what might be happening with others tended to arrive more quickly at a correct estimate of the situation.[73]

Part   II:
Impact

1.
The illusion of centrality

AT THE MOMENT of impact of a large-scale disaster there is a tendency for each individual involved to think that only he or only his house was hit. Under some circumstances this is the most likely assumption, until one gets further evidence. In other instances, the interpretation of the event as focused on oneself appears to be motivated by distorting subjective factors. Whatever the reasons for the initial mistaken impression, certain feelings are apt to be stimulated by the image of the event as centered on the self, which give way to other feelings as one becomes aware of the scope of the disaster.[74]

We are all familiar with upsets of limited extent, affecting only ourselves, or at most our households—illnesses, something going wrong with the furnace, and so on. When a disaster manifests itself by signs which in the usual course of life would indicate some such circumscribed disturbance, it seems natural to suppose that this is all there is to it, until one gets evidence to the contrary. So, for instance, in a factory where an odorless poison gas was escaping, each of the workers attributed his growing feelings of illness to some familiar cause, such as a hang-over, or not having eaten any breakfast.[75] Similarly, in a recent flood in England, among householders who began to see water seeping into their houses, "the first thought was that the situation related only to them: the taps were leaking, the pipes had burst, etc."[76] When a shipment of high explosives in a railway yard in South Amboy blew up, and houses were shaken and windows shattered for many blocks, those affected thought first that something had happened in their own house, that the furnace or the hot water boiler had exploded, for instance.[77]

While such interpretations are plausible in terms of past experience, people may also cling to them in the face of conflicting present evidence because they fear to acknowledge a more devastating reality. Thus a householder who has heard flood warnings may still try to assure himself that the water he sees on the floor was spilled by the children.[78] Here denial tendencies support the mistaken and circumscribed idea of what is happening.

At other times the nature of the event is correctly identified, but there is what we might call an illusion of centrality. The individual mistakenly supposes on subjective grounds that what has struck was more focused on himself than was actually the case. One form of this illusion would be what might be called the ground-zero effect: where a person imagines himself at the central point of contact of a destructive force, whose effect is pictured at the same time as radiating outwards from this center. He is not the exclusive target, but he is the focal one. In the case of bombing, for instance, each person who feels the blast may think that the bomb has fallen directly on his house or in his immediate neighborhood. When the atomic bomb fell on Hiroshima, a German missionary at some distance from the town had "the impression that it exploded directly over our house or in the immediate vicinity."[79] A woman outside Nagasaki said that when she saw the blinding flash, "I thought the bomb had hit right in front of me."[80] This illusion of centrality is the more extreme where it is believed that the damage is concentrated exclusively on the spot where one happens to be. Not only is one at the center, but one is the exclusive target: the rest of the world is unaffected. This reaction is frequently reported by tornado victims. As a survivor of the Worcester tornado put it: "I thought it was just something that happened to me."[81] Tornado victims whose houses have blown in on them often assume their house alone was hit.[82]

A number of factors probably contribute to this illusion of centrality. The large scale event, though nominally recognized, may still be assimilated to the model of more familiar circumscribed accidents. Also in undergoing a terrifying blow, the individual may tend to withdraw emotional interest from the rest of the world, concentrating it on his threatened self. The feeling that what has happened is exclusively confined to him may express this constriction of emotional concern. Conversely the assumption that nothing has happened to anyone else may reflect the temporary lack of interest in others. A man from Worcester who had crouched in terror on the floor of his truck as it was shaken and tossed by the tornado, and who said he thought it was something that happened only to him, tried to explain in this way why he failed in the time that followed to go to the assistance of others. In effect he tended to overlook patent signs of extensive damage. And he afterwards blamed the authorities for not having broadcast through loudspeakers the information which would have set him right and led him to be more helpful.[83] We may interpret such a reaction as one of incapacity to recognize what has happened to others because of the exclusive concentration of emotional energy on the self. I shall discuss this kind of reaction in more detail presently in connection with the extremes of egoism and altruism which a disaster evokes.

When one suffers a misfortune there is always the possibility, as we noted earlier, that one may take it as a punishment, construing one's relation to fate on the model of the child's relation to his parents. This susceptibility also may contribute to the illusion of being the sole victim to the extent that one thinks of punishment as meted out precisely and specifically to the one who has sinned. I shall also discuss later cultural variables in beliefs about individual or communal guilt which may affect such reactions. The tendency to assume that if I am punished, it is something that happens to me alone is apt to be facilitated by the kind of upbringing in which parents weigh the responsibility of the children involved, let us say, in a fight and single out one who was to blame, for instance, the one who started it. The experience that when I am punished my brothers are not may provide a model for feeling that if misfortune has fallen on me it is directed against me alone.

Perhaps another model for the illusion of centrality in disaster would be one according to which the family, rather than the individual, is singled out for misfortune. Many myths and much tragic literature relate stories of a family peculiarly cursed and suffering one fatality after another. The crimes for which the family is punished in this way are mainly those of murder or forbidden sex, corresponding more or less closely to the oedipal motives (in the fate of the house of Atreus, in Oedipus, in Hamlet, in Phèdre, etc.). The recurrent appeal of such stories derives from the fact that they deal with motives which family life repeatedly evokes. The readiness to believe that one's own family is peculiarly marked out for misfortune is related to guilt for unconscious feelings of hate and incestuous love within the family. The initial thought of the disaster victim that the disaster has fallen on his house alone may spring from the same source as tales of a family curse.

In the initial illusion of centrality in a damaging event there is an abrupt reversal of the usual pre-disaster assumption about one's own immunity. Before one is overtaken by a disaster, one tends to feel implicitly: something may happen to others, but nothing can happen to me. With the direct impact of a disastrous event, there is a sudden redistribution of immunity. One's own immunity has broken down, but one assumes that the rest of the world has remained intact.

The immediate expectation of the disaster victim who supposes that he alone, or only his family, has been hit is that the surrounding world, presumed to be unaffected, will come to his aid. As a tornado victim says: "I didn't realize it was everything (that was hit), and I thought, 'Why don't none of them come and help us?' "[84] Another woman in the same predicament says: "We just couldn't imagine that the whole town was destroyed, and I told my husband I said, 'Well, the rest of the town will be over here after us.' "[85] Another tornado victim relates: "I didn't realize anything had happened to anybody, only us . . . I said, 'Take me over to my sister's—she lives right next door.' And she said, 'Grandmother, we can't do that. Aunt Sarah doesn't have a home any more than you do. It's blown flat.' "[86]

Thus the victim of a large-scale disaster undergoes a second shock as he discovers that his initial interpretation was mistaken.[87] The surrounding world is no less damaged than himself; its expected resources for refuge and aid are sadly reduced. Insofar as the experience of disaster involves a painful sense of abandonment (an aspect which I shall go into in more detail presently), the discovery that the environment is not immediately available to help but is in its turn damaged and weakened, reenforces this feeling of being abandoned. The house next door in which one expected to be received and comforted has also been destroyed. The friends from the other side of town whom one expects to appear imminently full of solicitude are occupied with extricating themselves from the ruins of their own house.

At the same time the discovery of the extent of the damage may have certain reassuring effects. The feelings of culpability and of being punished which are apt to be associated with misfortunes confined to the self or the family are reduced. In an accident one is apt to blame oneself: One should have had enough foresight or control to avoid it; one is surrounded by people who have not had an accident. Insofar as such feelings may have been evoked by the illusion of centrality they are apt to be dispelled by realizing that one shares a common fate. The feeling about the distribution of strength between oneself and the environment may be reversed. In the initial phase one felt weakened while the environment seemed strong. As one sees others damaged as much or more than oneself (presuming that one is not physically incapacitated), one may feel a sense of returning or enhanced strength. From feeling helpless, one turns to helping others. The initial feeling that the damaging event may have been aimed particularly at oneself becomes dissipated. So, for instance, an Italian earthquake victim, while she thought that her house had fallen in on her because of a peculiar flaw or because someone had put a curse on it, was in such despair that she wanted to die in the wreckage. When, however, she learned about the earthquake, she became quite cheerful and began making plans to rebuild her house.[88] Thus the discovery that one has not been singled out for misfortune tends to reduce distress.

Where an initial impression of an event of limited scope has given way to acknowledgment of extended damage, there is often a tendency to exaggerate its proportions. Immediately following a disastrous event there are apt to be rumors of much greater destruction and particularly more loss of life than actually occurred.[89] We may see in this the tendency towards exaggeration which often constitutes a phase in the acceptance of a painful reality.[90] One compensates for an initial underestimation by a subsequent overestimation, oscillating between extremes before one gets the correct picture. Probably in many cases there are repeated alternations of too much and too little. Among the spectators at the race track at Le Mans, immediately following the catastrophe in which a racing car crashed into the crowd, there were rapidly shifting rumors that twenty had been killed, one hundred, fifty, and so on.[91] A terrible event also stimulates destructive fantasies, which may take the form of overestimation of damage. Often in a disaster-stricken community there are false rumors of the death of particular individuals.[92] One may suppose that latent hostile wishes help to give rise to such beliefs, while positive feelings are also present towards those who have thus been killed off in imagination. The presumed dead ones are welcomed all the more warmly when they turn up alive because negative feelings towards them have been so fully gratified in believing them dead.

2.

The feeling of abandonment

A FEELING of being abandoned probably plays a major part in the emotional distress of a disastrous experience. This feeling has its roots in early childhood. The small child becomes anxious when mother is away because he is helpless to satisfy his own needs and is in danger of being overwhelmed by distressing feelings which he cannot himself alleviate.[93] Later danger situations are apt to reactivate the feelings related to earlier ones. The sense of helplessness in the impact of a disastrous event throws the individual back into the childhood position.[94] All his vital needs are threatened with frustration and his acquired capacity to take care of himself is set aside by an overpowering force. Being alone in such a situation is likely to be particularly devastating. The presence of others, especially beloved persons, who are often embraced at such times, may help to counteract the feeling of abandonment. But I would suggest that this feeling is very frequently present in some degree in the disaster victim at the moment of impact. Disaster calls up feelings about the individual's relations to fate which are often latent in more quiet times. One is apt to assume without thinking that fate, the gods, whoever presides over the course of events, is well disposed, on one's side, arranging things on the whole favorably. When one is suddenly overtaken by catastrophe there is an awful feeling of having been deserted by this protective power: why hast Thou forsaken me?

A young man whose house was destroyed by a tornado speaks of how he felt immediately afterwards: "You feel like you've lost your best friend." And his wife says: "You just feel completely lost."[95] Another tornado survivor, a young man who saw his father killed in a collapsing building, says: "It's a helpless lost feeling." He expresses his sense of personal loss in speaking of the transformation of the familiar friendly environment: "I've lived in this little town all my life. I mean, I was actually lost. I didn't know where I was at because there were no landmarks, nothing to go by."[96] The death of loved persons is often felt unconsciously as a desertion. Thus the death of someone near to oneself greatly intensifies the feeling of abandonment already stimulated by the very fact that the disaster could happen. The transformation of the physical environment which one knew and loved also has the effect of a desertion. The young man is no longer at home in his home town, he is lost. We use the word "lost" equally for someone who cannot find his way in a strange place and for a child separated from his parents. A woman who, on emerging from the ruins of her house after a tornado and, seeing the whole neighborhood laid waste, thought she must be the sole survivor says: "It's the loneliest feeling in the world."[97] Another woman expresses her intense anxiety and sense of loss of everything good and protective in a disaster, again that of a tornado: "You have such an insecure feeling. . . . You don't feel secure anywhere, with anybody or anything."[98]

The feeling of abandonment, of loss of the protection usually assumed to be present in the environment, is likely to be evoked by the impact of a disaster regardless of the specific deprivations which one or another individual suffers. Naturally each disaster victim will express this sense of loss in terms of his particular experience. For one the loss of his home is like losing one's best friend; for another the impression of being a solitary survivor is the "loneliest feeling in the world," and so on.

Contact or lack of contact with others in the impact of a catastrophe can mitigate or aggravate the feeling of abandonment. A woman who was trapped in the basement of a devastated department store building, in which she had been working when a tornado struck, says: "I thought all the time that the rest had escaped and gone home and just left me there, and didn't know I was pinned down in that basement there like I was, and that they had gone home."[99] In such instances the separation from others intensifies the feeling of being deserted and the absent ones may be reproached with having left one to one's fate. The absence of a loved person in moments of extremity may be hard to forgive. A little girl who had been separated from her father during a tornado afterwards hit him angrily, reproaching him for having been away from her.[100] A woman who was separated from her son at the moment of impact finds this so painful in retrospect that at one point in her retelling of the experience she changes her story to say: "We was both standing right together . . . and he had his arms around my waist, the last I remember anything." She then again recalls the details more exactly, how her son had gone into the bedroom to put on a shirt, how the bedroom had then been blown away, and "that was the last time I knew where I was at. I was right there by myself."[101]

The mistaken expectation that others should be immediately available to come to one's aid, based on the illusion of centrality which we have already discussed, adds to the feeling of abandonment. As the same woman put it, after her house had been destroyed and she and her son injured: "See, we didn't have no place to go. Wasn't no one ever come over there and seen about us or nothing."[102]

The sentiment of the hymn, "Abide with me, fast falls the eventide," is strongly felt in extreme situations, and attaches both to human and to superhuman presences. A woman who was together with her fifteen-year-old daughter when a tornado struck recounts her experience: "And she said, 'Mother, it's coming—a cyclone.' And I said, 'Mary, I'm afraid it is. But,' I said, 'we're together.' And she said, 'Mother, I love you and we're together.' I shall never forget those words. And we—our arms were around each other, and I said, 'Whatever happens, Mary, let's cling together.' "[103] This scene may have been a bit improved upon in the retelling. But in any case it expresses the longing for physical and emotional closeness as protection against the feeling of abandonment. The great boon to a disaster victim of having someone promise to stay with him is illustrated in the following episode. Two injured men were trying to crawl out of a burning plant following the explosion in Texas City. As one of them, who had suffered a broken leg, puts it: "Then Johnny and Clyde came along. I said, 'Johnny, help us—we can't walk.' His arms were broken, and he said, 'I can't help you, but I'll stay with you. If you can crawl, I'll guide you.' Talk about cheer! That helped me more than anything—just when he said, 'I'll stay with you.' "[104]

Disaster victims, looking back on their experience, often stress their intense feelings of love for others and the great goodness of others towards themselves in the time following the event. I would suggest that this creation of a loving world derives part of its impetus from an immediately preceding phase in which the feeling was just the opposite, namely, that of being abandoned by the world. Every gesture of help takes on an enhanced value as it rescues the individual from the loneliness into which the disaster has precipitated him. There is such a need to be reassured that one has not been utterly deserted that any help one receives assumes great emotional significance. A devastating situation is reversed: it is like a lost child finding his mother again. I think that the feeling of abandonment which precedes the feeling of being so warmly embraced by the human community has probably been played down in retrospect by disaster victims, who are anxious to assure themselves: it was really not so bad as I thought in the worst moments. Disaster researchers have also tended to overlook the feeling of abandonment, stressing rather the sense of human solidarity following a disaster.[105] In this the researchers show the common reluctance of the outsider to put himself in the place of the sufferer. Intolerance for painful feelings may thus lead researchers and their subjects to collaborate in neglecting certain aspects of a disastrous experience.

An intensification of religious faith sometimes appears following a disaster. I would suggest that this reenforced belief may be in part a reaction to a moment of doubt when the disaster struck. Just as a warm faith in humanity succeeds the feeling of abandonment, so a sense of closeness to God may follow upon the feeling that He has withdrawn His protection in leaving one a prey to the disastrous event. Freud speaks of an experience of loss of faith in which an individual, confronted with a sight which conflicted with his antecedent ideas of what ought and what ought not to happen in the world, felt: if this can happen, God does not exist. This loss of faith may then be followed by an experience of intensified contact with God.[106] The mechanism involved in this reversal is far from clear. Where the need for a protective power is very great, there is apt to be an effort to construe even the most disastrous events in a way compatible with the existence of such a power. A woman, for instance, who had seen her little girl killed by a plane which crashed into a crowd of spectators, after a phase of paralyzing grief had a sudden consoling revelation of her little girl being happy with God, who had chosen to take her to Himself because she was too good for this world.[107] Evidently we touch here on the well known "problem of evil" which has so often troubled theologians. I shall go into this more later in connection with a variety of post-disaster reactions to the powers that be. What I mainly wish to bring out at this time is the sequence of polarized feelings of abandonment and togetherness which attend a disaster, and which may be expressed in terms of both human and superhuman relations.

In a danger situation where the isolation of the individual has been enforced by special sanctions, an occasion of friendly contact with others may evoke highly euphoric feelings even though the danger remains extreme. Thus Bettelheim speaks of an experience in a German concentration camp, where ordinarily any demonstration of fellow-feeling among the prisoners was interfered with by severe penalties. On one occasion the prisoners, subjected to the torture of standing all night in the freezing cold, ceased to care what happened to them and dared, as they usually would not have, to help each other. Their sense of solidarity temporarily freed them from fear and gave them a feeling of rare happiness.[108]

For young children the feeling of abandonment in a disaster situation depends very much on whether they are with their parents or not, and whether their parents continue to appear strong and protective. The trust in protective powers has not yet been displaced from the parents to fate or some other more large-scale agency. The child tends to feel safe as long as he is with his parents, whose powers of control over the world he of course overestimates. If his parents leave him for more than a brief time, he is subject in any case to feelings of anxiety and to fantasies of being abandoned, and these become the more intensified if he has to undergo other frightening experiences. Where a child is together with his parents in a danger situation, but where the parents become sufficiently alarmed to reveal their feeling of helplessness to cope with the danger, the child also experiences frightened feelings of abandonment. The image of the parents as all-powerful protectors breaks down. The extent to which young children's reactions to a danger situation depends on whether they are with their parents, and on how their parents take it, has been substantiated by many observations.[109]

The presence of a trusted leader in an organized group (as in an army unit in war time) has a similar effect of seeming to assure protection to his followers. The appearance of calm and confidence in the leader suggests to the followers that it is he who copes directly with the danger, that he intervenes between it and themselves. Where the leader loses this appearance of control, the followers may become filled with alarm that the force of the danger is about to strike them directly.[110] The presence of authority figures in a city under-going bombing contributes to the citizens' feelings of being protected. Where such personages leave the city, those left behind are likely to feel abandoned. The increased anxiety which ensues may be complicated by the feeling that such abandonment is a punishment (in effect: I must have been bad if my parents turn away from me). This stimulation of a sense of guilt in turn releases further alarm because of the anticipation of possible further punishment.[111] Also, if the elite escape to safety those who are left behind may feel that liability to danger and death is limited to low and insignifi-cant persons. Self-disparaging tendencies may be strengthened by such circumstances; the individual may feel that he is un-worthy of being saved. Being abandoned by parent surrogates in a danger situation may have other disturbing effects. So, for instance, in London during the Blitz, some who remained tried to inhibit their resentment against admired persons (for instance, their doctor) who left the city by saying that this departure was really justified by the extremity of the danger. Having made this excuse for the abandoning ones, they then became increasingly fearful of the danger which they had thus been led to magnify.[112]

The feeling of abandonment which a disaster tends to arouse intensifies the anxiety about loved ones from whom one is separated and who may be in the danger zone. Evi-dently there are realistic grounds for apprehension about loved persons in such circumstances. But I would suggest that the sense of loss which the very occurrence of the disas-ter is apt to evoke reenforces this anxiety. Persons seeking reassurance about the fate of their relatives (and this applies also to those coming in from outside the disaster zone) often find merely verbal reports inadequate. They must see and touch those from whom the disaster threatened to separate them forever before their anxiety begins to be assuaged.[113] We find it natural that people who have been apart during a disaster should embrace each other when they come together afterwards. I think that this urge towards physical contact represents in part a revival of early childhood feelings about separation. The little child who is crying for his absent mother is not consoled by mere verbal assurances that mother is coming soon. He has become unsure whether the mother who has gone away, who is not there when he wants her so desperately, still exists. It is necessary for him to see her and to be held close to her again for his apprehension of an irretrievable separation to be overcome.

The intensification of separation anxiety which a disaster produces often persists for some time after the event. Thus we find children staying closer to mother than they had before, parents feeling uneasy at having their children out of their sight, and both children and adults sometimes showing anxiety about going out of the house.[114] These reactions are also related to the frequent fear of an imminent recurrence of the disaster.

3.
Near- and remote-miss

/\

THERE ARE different degrees of exposure to a catastrophic event: one may be nearer to, or farther from the center of extreme danger. I would use the term "objective near-miss" for the situation of the individual in the danger zone for whom there is a considerable degree of probability of personal damage, for instance if one is in a house that is destroyed by a bomb, a tornado, or an earthquake. Correspondingly an "objective remote-miss" would refer to a position outside the area of such acute threat but sufficiently proximate that those so situated feel some relation of the disaster to themselves. I would distinguish further what I would call "subjective near- and remote-misses." A "subjective near-miss" is an experience in which the individual's sense of invulnerability is shattered. His usual feeling that nothing can happen to him gives way to the sudden terrible apprehension that he is about to suffer a devastating loss, of beloved objects, of physical intactness, of life itself. A "subjective remote-miss" would refer to an experience of danger in which the sense of invulnerability is preserved. We may suppose that being in an objective near-miss siuation is likely to produce a subjective near-miss experience, and that conversely physical remoteness from the danger would be more

(65)

apt to be associated with a subjective remote-miss reaction. However, different individual susceptibilities make for variations in response: the same situation which shatters one person's feeling of invulnerability may leave another's intact.

There is some evidence to suggest that a subjective near-miss experience is associated with subsequent emotional disturbances. Where, on the other hand, the exposure to danger has not disrupted the individual's confidence in his invulnerability, such disturbance is less likely to occur.[115] Thus psychiatric casualties among bomber personnel in the last war said that in the moment of extreme danger they had the thought that they could die more often than those who came out of the same experiences emotionally unimpaired. The latter more frequently preserved through the hazards they underwent the conviction of their own invulnerability.[116] A related finding is that complete loss of consciousness in a situation of extreme danger where the individual is helpless may facilitate surviving without emotional damage. After the Cocoanut Grove fire, when the survivors who manifested severe emotional disturbances were compared with those who did not (physical injuries and loss of loved ones being equated for the two groups), there was found to be a significant difference in this respect. There had been a higher incidence and a longer duration of loss of consciousness during the fire on the part of those who afterwards did not manifest psychiatric complications.[117] A subjective near-miss experience was here avoided by the exclusion of the threatening stimuli from consciousness.

Thus, in the moment of direct exposure to danger it would seem that a certain degree of denial, to the extent of preserving the illusion of personal invulnerability, acts as a protection against emotional impairment. The breakdown of this illusion in a devastating sense of one's own vulnerability is apt to be followed by emotional disturbances.

A number of factors may make for susceptibility to a subjective near-miss reaction. To the extent to which an individual retains infantile fantasies of omnipotence he is more likely to feel overwhelmed by events going drastically counter to his wishes. Latent castration anxiety, in the sense of exaggerated fear of injury or uncertainty about one's physical adequacy, is likely to be activated by exposure to danger. Since belief in the existence or maintenance of one's own intactness is already weak, it is the more easily shaken by the occurrence of injury or a narrow escape from it. Guilt feelings are similarly conducive to an impaired sense of invulnerability, as one is haunted by apprehensions of the punishment which one feels one deserves. When one is then overtaken by catastrophe the anticipated punishment appears to have materialized. It has been suggested that facing real dangers may have a reassuring effect when the real turns out to be less terrible than the imagined danger.[118] This may be supposed to operate in the experience of a subject remote-miss. In the subjective near miss on the other hand the actual danger seems to coincide with, or exceed, the imagined one. Survival fails to have a reassuring effect: the individual's sense of security is shattered.

As we would expect, the individual's attitude towards further dangers corresponds to whether he has experienced a subjective near- or remote-miss. While the subjective near-miss anticipates a possible renewed danger with great apprehensiveness, the remote-miss is apt to feel increased confidence. His survival of the past danger is taken as confirming his invulnerability.[119] The expectation of whether further damaging events are likely to occur or not varies in a similar way. The near-miss, having lost faith in his luck, is the one who expects further misfortune. Here again the tendency to take disaster as punishment enters in. But the near- and remote-miss interpret in different ways the punishment which they may both feel they have undergone. For the remote-miss there is the feeling that he has paid and is now in the clear. This is as if to say: you cannot be tried twice for the same crime. It is related to such folk beliefs as that lightning never strikes twice in the same place. For the near-miss, the punishment which the disaster may be felt to represent is only a beginning, a warning of more to come. The punishing powers have declared their intent to pursue him and may be expected to continue relentlessly. This feeling is expressed in such folk sayings as "never two without three" as applied to expected sequences of misfortune.

We might expect subjective near-miss reactions in circumstances of suffering physical injury, being in a building (or ship, or plane) which is damaged, the death of a family member (or other person to whom one is closely attached, such as a wartime buddy), being rendered homeless, and being exposed to the sight of dead and injured.[120] In the absence of such direct experiences, the occurrence of a subjective near-miss reaction would appear to be more pathological. To the extent that a physically remote danger can shatter the individual's confidence in his invulnerability, this confidence must already have been weak, due to such factors as we have already noted (e.g. castration anxiety, guilt feelings). We may make an analogy here between those who are apprehensive about threats which are remote in time and those who become seriously disturbed about disasters which occur at some distance from them in space. The readiness to react to such remote events suggests an antecedent state of emotional disturbance.

Following the Worcester tornado one of the very few psychiatric casualties recorded was a woman whose house was on the periphery of the tornado's path but who seems to have suffered a near-miss reaction.[121] At any rate she acknowledges that she is occupied afterwards with thoughts of what might have happened "if we'd been right plunk in the middle of it, right in that whirling section of it." Thus she seems unable to accept the immunity vouchsafed her in the actual event, but feels impelled to imagine herself and her family in an objective near-miss position. The intensity of her reaction suggests that the imagined hazards carry with them a subjective near-miss effect. A hypothetical reconstruction of some of the factors which seem to have been involved here may indicate the kinds of antecedent disturbances which contribute to such disproportionate reactions.

At the time the tornado struck, Mrs. T. was very angry with her husband. She characterizes herself as generally sickly and timid. The violent storm made her apprehensive and she wanted the family to go down to the cellar, but her husband was slow to share her alarm. He may well have been in the habit of pooh-poohing her apprehensions. Afterwards, in speaking of her husband, Mrs. T. is very mocking about his pretensions to know better. Despite the fact that he has a lot of weather forecasting equipment, he did not recognize ahead of time the nature of the storm. Perhaps, says his wife, "he's not educated enough in the weather to know." In any case, she seems to have felt misunderstood and unprotected by her husband in her anxiety at the height of the storm. Such lack of emotional contact contributes to the feeling of abandonment which we have previously discussed. Following the tornado, Mr. T. went out to help in the rescue activities and did not return until three or four in the morning. Mrs. T. suffered severe anxiety during his absence: "He was out ... and I was all alone with my children ... I couldn't sleep, I couldn't sleep till he got in the house." We do not of course know to what extent Mrs. T. was subject to such reactions to her husband's being away at night in more normal times. Her intense anxiety on this occasion, besides being related to real or imagined dangers hovering over the disaster area, probably reflected her feeling of having been abandoned in the moment of impact, her rage against her husband, and her resentment of his giving help to others. Anxiety in the absence of a loved person is, as we know, often related to repressed hostile feelings towards him.

The next day Mrs. T. felt impelled to make a special trip to buy her husband a present. In anticipation of Father's Day, she set out in the car with her little girl to go to a shop some distance away. But now another, smaller catastrophe occurred. Mrs. T. failed to notice the water meter or temperature gauge on the car. To her alarm the engine began to emit smoke. She stopped the car, jumped out, and, excited and tearful, ran into a nearby house to ask that they call the fire department. As it eventually appeared the car was simply out of water. But Mrs. T. was too distraught to continue on her trip. As she says, "I just wanted to get back home as fast as I could." Possibly she had already felt uneasy about leaving home when she set out. Now she had succeeded in precipitating an incident which produced intense anxiety about being away from home. When, with considerable reluctance, she told her husband what had happened, he scolded her for her lack of observancy about the car and the damage which she had caused. Mrs. T. had felt up until this point that it had not been her fault. In response to her husband's reproaches, she started to cry. "And I cried and I cried, and then all of a sudden everything went black."

Through the course of this episode Mrs. T. seems to be agitated by intense ambivalence towards her husband. She attempts to exclude from awareness, and to act counter to her hostile feelings towards him, which were aggravated by his desertion, as she felt it, during the disaster and following it, and by the possibility that something might happen to him, which was suggested by the many fatalities so close at hand. Thus she tries, in her reaction against her hostility, to do something especially nice for him. But because of her negative feelings she is unable to accomplish this. Rather, through what would seem to have been a motivated oversight, she does damage to the car (thus indirectly to her husband). She still makes a desperate effort to conceal from herself that this was her fault (the garage man should have checked the car, etc.). When her husband blames her for damaging the car, it becomes very difficult for her to continue to exclude from awareness the feelings of hostility towards him which she has been trying to repress. It is as if in blaming her about the car, her husband is saying: look, you are really damaging me. She is forced to blank out consciousness in a fainting fit to prevent herself from becoming aware of the destructive impulses which she cannot accept. Or perhaps in falling into a deathlike faint, she turns back upon herself the hostile tendencies which a guilty awareness diverts from their external object. The material here is of course very incomplete, and the interpretations therefore quite tentative.

Death wishes towards a loved person, stimulated by the

closeness of danger, may boomerang under the pressure of guilt feelings. The person who in the sight of damage thinks about his loved and hated spouse: why not her? is apt to be struck very soon with the retaliatory thought: why not me? This then might be one of a number of predisposing conditions for readiness to experience a subjective near-miss reaction even in an objective remote-miss situation.

The distress of such a bystander may also be related to guilt for failing to help those who have seriously suffered in the disaster.[122] Helpful activities in such circumstances have the effect of strengthening the individual's faith in his own goodness. Where he is unable to help he may feel that he is in effect acquiescing in the destruction, which is an external counterpart to his own bad impulses. Indeed, the preponderance of destructive impulses within the individual may, as in the case just cited, incapacitate him from working to undo the effects of external destruction.

The person whose family is in the danger zone while he is outside it evidently suffers extreme anxiety about his loved ones, which is also complicated by feelings about not sharing the danger with them. However much one loves another person, it is not quite easy to give a simple and wholeheartedly affirmative answer to the question: if a choice were given, would I die to save him? Orwell in his *Nineteen-eighty-four* evokes a situation where the hero, threatened with an unbearably frightening torture, feels impelled to offer up the woman he loves instead, and suddenly shouts: "Do it to her!" His torturers have thus succeeded in disillusioning him with his capacity for love. Whatever suspicion the person outside the danger situation may have in this way of any inclination in himself to prefer the death of his loved ones to his own annihilation must provoke feelings of guilt and unworthiness. Guilt feelings in such a situation are of course also stimulated by hostile wishes towards the loved ones, which may have been experienced at any time in the past, wishes that now to one's extreme distress seem about to come true. The threat of gratification of the negative sector of the ambivalence towards loved persons leads to an intensification of the positive sector: one feels that one never loved them as much as now, when one is confronted with the possibility of losing them.

The feelings of guilt of the person who rushes back from outside the disaster zone to look for his endangered family may also lead to apprehensions of retribution. A man who was away from home when his town was struck by a tornado tells of his feelings on his way back to his family: "I expected the worst, you know. You couldn't—driving a little bit fast—even think. I had to watch the road. I had to watch what few cars were behind me and I didn't give it too much thought ... I only had one thought in mind and that was to get there and get there in one piece—get under all those wires... That same thing was on my mind all the way in—to get there in one piece—not have a wreck or hit anything, run into any of these wires. I was rather careful. I watched what I did."[123] Thus, struggling with his fears for his family, this man tries to exclude from consciousness the thought that they may all be killed. Instead he becomes preoccupied with the idea of an accident that could happen to him on the way back. This anxiety about himself was no doubt due in large part to the hazards of the road. But it seems possible that it was also intensified by guilt at not sharing his family's fate, and the thought: something should happen to me. The motive of sacrifice may also have entered in: if I am damaged, they will be saved. The fates might accept one victim in place of another. The counterpart of these thoughts in consciousness was the idea, fraught with anxiety, that something might happen to himself and that he must exercise the utmost vigilance to prevent it.

Those on the periphery of the disaster area, even if they do not have relatives or friends in the impact zone, are affected in various ways by the proximity of the event. In general, we react differently to an event if it happens close to us than if it happens far away, even if we are not involved and are not in a position to do anything about it. This is a commonplace observation, but the reaction is not entirely easy to explain. It would seem that the readiness for empathy, for imagining oneself in the situation one hears or reads about, varies with physical distance. So with a disaster, if one hears about it from hundreds of miles away, one usually has little sense of having escaped a hazard and little feeling that it could have happened to oneself. Those on the periphery of the disaster area cannot feel that unaffected. They are rather apt to be torn between a distressing feeling that it could have happened to them, and the wish to maintain their usual comfortable sense of immunity.

People on the outskirts of the disaster area are usually impelled to go in and see what has happened and to see if there is anything that they can do. I shall discuss later in more detail the motive of looking at scenes of destruction, and also the manifestations of altruism following a disaster. What I wish to bring out in the present context is the conflict of the person into whose vicinity such an event has intruded about his own relation to it. A young man in a college just outside Waco at the time when it was hit by a tornado tells of how hard it was for him to decide whether to go into the city or not after he had heard of the disaster. As he and his friends decided to go, they were able to observe in gradual stages the signs of devastation. That is, they had an advantage over the person in the impact zone of being able to dose their exposure to the damage. The objective near-miss is overwhelmed with traumatic stimuli which he must struggle to master subsequently. The objective remote-miss has more control over his exposure to distressing stimuli. Reluctantly and one step at a time he takes in the extent of what has happened. The near-miss becomes aware in the moment of impact of the threat to life itself, and only subsequently, as he takes stock of the environment, recognizes the extent of property damage. The perception of the remote-miss proceeds in the opposite direction. Moving into the disaster zone (in the case of explosive disasters such as tornadoes or bombings), he first notices material destruction: trees uprooted, wrecked cars, and so on. Unwillingly and painfully he acknowledges that this much damage has been done before he confronts the realization of loss of life.

The same Texas college boy speaks of the further shock, when he and his friends got to the center of the devastated city, of seeing many buildings leveled to the ground and being forced to infer that there must be dead people under the ruins. At this point, as he puts it: "I felt kind of, somewhat like I was out of place."[124] Thus with magnificent inarticulateness and understatement, the young man expresses, in terms more appropriate to a slight social embarrassment, the sense of protest which he felt, in his youth and vigor, at finding himself so close to death. His sense of invulnerability is threatened by this proximity and he would like to get away, to get back to the feeling he had such a short time ago that such catastrophe could have nothing to do with him. As he says: "I was surprised that I myself was as close as I was to such a thing." At the same time it is difficult to ward off the suggestion, which physical closeness seems to convey, that it could have happened to him.

The young man then tried to get rid of the distressing feelings roused by this contact with fatality by throwing himself actively into the work of clearing away the rubble. He felt, as he puts it, "a little nervousness that I needed to work off by doing something." The tendency to imagine himself in the place of the victims is counteracted by strenuous activity which gives the reassurance that he is not damaged but strong and able. I shall add other observations later about the motives and effects of strenuous activity in the immediate post-disaster phase. In the case of this rescuer who came in from outside, let me only add that he did not participate directly in the unearthing of any of the corpses: "No, I didn't dig anyone out, thank goodness." Another young man in the same situation tells of his impulse towards flight after contact with the dead: "I dug out a body with some of the boys up there and it kinda threw me. So I thought, well, I'd go home and get away from it."[125] There would seem to be something like a sense of magic of contiguity in such reactions: an unconscious apprehension that damage and death may be catching if one gets too close.

The tendency to feel guilty on the part of the person whose

family is in danger while he is not has already been mentioned. Such feelings are also apt to occur, though with less intensity, in those on the periphery towards victims who are strangers.[126] The feeling that one is glad it is the other and not oneself evokes some compunction even in relation to people whom one does not know. Also, since on the unconscious level there is apt to be a belief in the power of the dead to revenge themselves on the living, there may be a fear that those to whose death one consents (in the thought: rather him than me) will retaliate. The impulse, to which there is also strong resistance, to imagine oneself in the place of the victims may have in part an expiatory motive, as if by a token suffering and death in imagination one pays for one's guilt towards the dead and purchases immunity to retaliation.

4.

The disaster syndrome

.\/

IN DISASTER VICTIMS immediately after the event a certain combination of reactions has frequently been observed: absence of emotion, lack of response to present stimuli, inhibition of outward activity, docility, undemandingness. Observers repeatedly describe persons in this state as "stunned," "dazed," "shocked." Wallace has named this the "disaster syndrome."[127]

An observer in the great earthquake at Messina in 1909 reported: "The immediate and almost universal effect that the earthquake had on those who escaped death at Messina was of stupefaction, almost of mental paralysis. They were stunned . . . Lamentation was infrequently heard except when caused by physical suffering. Tears were rarely seen. Men recounted how they had lost wife, mother, brothers, sisters, children, and all their possessions, with no apparent concern. They told their tales of woe as if they themselves had been disinterested spectators of another's loss."[128] A witness at Hiroshima described "the silence in the grove by the river, where hundreds of gruesomely wounded suffered together. . . . The hurt ones were quiet; no one wept, much less screamed in pain; no one complained; none of the many who died did so noisily; not even the children cried; very few people even spoke."[129]

In a series of Middle Western tornadoes, "with almost monotonous regularity the survivors in the zone of destruction were described as appearing 'stunned,' 'dazed,' or 'shocked.' "[130] A man coming into a tornado-stricken town just after the disaster reported: "They (the survivors) were orderly. There wasn't anybody unduly excited or hysterical. At first they were somewhat stunned, like—well, 'It couldn't happen, it just couldn't happen to us.' "[131] A tornado victim puts it: "Everybody was just in kind of a daze there for several days. They didn't know which way to turn or nothing, you know. ... Somebody would come along and tell me what they thought I ought to do. ... I didn't know what to do myself."[132]

Unawareness of injuries is often reported, and similarly unresponsiveness to external stimuli. A doctor in Worcester tells of an injured woman whom he approached amid the ruins following the tornado: "She didn't complain of pain. But I told her I was a doctor, and I had to get right up close to her and talk right into her ear because she was just moving around aimlessly ... out of contact more or less."[133] Tyhurst estimates that a majority of disaster victims (his observations being based on fires and flood) are stunned and bewildered, without conscious emotion though manifesting physical changes appropriate to fear, and with restricted awareness. (According to Tyhurst, minorities at opposite ends of the scale are calm, lucid and practical, or paralyzed by anxiety, crying hysterically, disoriented.)[134]

Let us try to reconstruct the dynamics of the state thus indicated. A number of factors would seem to be involved. For one thing, there is a tendency to deny what has happened. This may be expressed in manifest feelings of unreality. As one tornado victim put it: "We all just felt like it hasn't really happened—it's just a nightmare—it's just something that will be gone."[135] The inhibition of emotional response, as we have noted before, has the effect of denying the reality of the event: if I don't react to it, it doesn't exist. At the same time there is a fear of being overwhelmed by painful feelings once one begins to react to what has happened. The traumatic event is apt to be mastered gradually, as the individual allows himself little by little to respond to one or another detail of what he has experienced (as if a film were being developed one section at a time). The disaster victim attempts to keep the too intensive stimuli to which he has been subjected under control retroactively, dosing himself with as much as he can tolerate. There is frequently an intense fright reaction several days afterwards: the individual has prepared himself for it in the meantime.

Since the disaster victim has been forced to take in more than he can for the moment assimilate, his energies become engrossed in the task of mastering, of gradually inuring himself to the sudden and terrible experience. With this preoccupation, there is a resistance to taking in any more stimuli. The organism has been flooded with stimuli; it has not the capacity to accept more for the time being. Hence the insensitivity of the disaster victim to what is going on around him.

The unawareness of wounds is another denial, for the purpose of warding off overwhelming alarm and distress. Another related reaction is fainting, which may occur in the impact of the disaster, or sometimes days later when the overwhelming threat of the danger situation is about to emerge belatedly into consciousness.

As to the inhibition of activity, it has been suggested that this is related to the loss of usual cues, the shattering of the familiar environmental setting in which one knows how to act.[136] This factor would be decisive mainly for those who have been only slightly affected. Those, on the other hand, whose energies are absorbed in the task of mastering the traumatic experience are apt to be, as we have noted, relatively unresponsive to further external stimuli. For the same reason they have little energy free for outward action.

If we consider the combination of emotional dullness, unresponsiveness to outer stimulation, and inhibition of activity, and ask what familiar clinical syndrome it suggests, I think the answer would be that it most resembles what is observed in depression. We have already mentioned several factors which would be conducive to a depressive reaction in disaster. The individual's assumption of his own omnipotence, of the likelihood of the world's going the way he wants it to, is brusquely thrust aside by the occurrence of the disastrous event. The expectation of beneficent supplies from a loving environment is frustrated: the powers that rule the world seem to have abandoned the disaster victim. Further there may be the feeling that what has happened is a punishment, that the individual must have deserved it. All these factors are destructive of the individual's self-esteem. There is the feeling: I cannot be much good if this could happen to me; I am not omnipotent, nor lovable, nor virtuous.[137] The individual who has just undergone a disaster is thus apt to suffer from at least a transitory sense of worthlessness; his usual capacity for self-love becomes impaired.

Different individuals, depending on their antecedent emotional tendencies, will be more or less susceptible to this post-disaster depression. For those whose illusions of omnipotence are pronounced, or whose demands for external supplies are exorbitant, or who are already burdened with guilt feelings, the impact of a disaster might be expected to produce a more serious depression than in others. Probably in the "normal" case the post-disaster depression is transitory, being often followed by elation, as we shall see. We might contrast post-disaster depression with pathological depression in the following way, in respect, for instance, to the need for external supplies which is generally considered of central importance in depression.[138] In the pathologically depressed person the need for incessant manifestations of love from the environment is greater than can be satisfied in ordinary life; frustration and despair are thus unavoidable. In the case of the disaster victim, we have a situation of unusual deprivation in which at the same time the individual's needs for outside support become much greater than usual because of his sudden helplessness. Insofar as the disaster victim's depression is mainly a response to this exceptional situation, it is likely to be temporary.

The docility of disaster victims is related to factors already mentioned. As the disaster victim suffers from an inhibition

of his capacity for outward action he becomes dependent on
the initiative of others. Insofar as he interprets the disaster
as a punishment, he may respond like a severely beaten child
by becoming subdued and docile.[139] A trauma may be taken
in this way as a command, as an effort of the bludgeoning
powers to make one do what they require.[140] In response, the
disaster victim is apt to become not only docile but also, as
we shall see, extraordinarily good.

Disaster victims who have been physically injured have
been observed to be exceptionally quiet and undemanding.
As I have mentioned, they often do not seem to feel any
pain. Frequently they ask hospital attendants to take care of
others first, to take care of those who need it more. Hospital
personnel have remarked on the striking difference between
disaster victims and accident victims in this respect: the latter are apt to be demanding, complaining, excited, and clamorous.[141] Apparently there is an important difference between
undergoing isolated damage and being one among many
similarly affected. The disaster victim has, as we have seen,
undergone an intense experience of abandonment: not only
has he been damaged and deprived but he has seen the surrounding world devastated so that it could not immediately
come to his aid. By the time he has been taken to the hospital
he has a sense of the world beginning to be restored, of its
capacity and willingness to help him being once more in
effect. He is tremendously grateful. This is a repeated observation of rescuers: disaster victims are exceedingly apprecia-
tive of anything that is done for them, any gesture of helpfulness. We have noted already that this strong emotional
response to help is related to the antecedent feeling of abandonment. The recovery from the feeling of abandonment
involves both intense response to others' kindness and out-
going affection towards others. With the beginning of recovery of the world that seemed lost, there is a tendency for a
great feeling of affection to go out towards others in affirma-
tion of their existence: they are there after all, and one is not
alone.[142] The accident victim has not had the same experience

of the world destroyed and restored. He is less grateful for others' help: it is the least they can do, being in perfect shape, while he alone is damaged.

In many painful experiences, including accidents, suffering is aggravated by the fact that it is undergone alone. This often involves feelings of distance from others, who are not similarly affected, and hostility towards them. In a disaster, following the early phase of feeling abandoned, there is the discovery that others have undergone similar suffering and losses in the same event. Thus one has not been singled out for misfortune. A burden shared seems less hard to bear. The realization that one does not suffer alone is apt to occasion warm fellow-feeling towards other victims. The complaints of the accident victim are in part related to resentment against the rest of the world for being untouched. In a disaster, on the other hand, one need not contrast oneself with others to one's own disadvantage. Rather the situation of widespread damage can be utilized to find others worse off than oneself, and so to feel lucky by comparison (a circumstance which, as we shall see, seems to be particularly valued by Americans because of their peculiarly strong unwillingness to consider themselves unlucky). Also there is the feeling that one has no right to complain where so many others have suffered too, and are perhaps much worse off.[148] An anti-complaint morale springs up, as if to complain would be to show inadequate respect for the distress of others. We have already noted the tendency of the disaster victim to scotomize his own injuries. Surrounded by other victims, he can support his need to deny his own wounds by acknowledging theirs: take care of them, they are worse off than I. Concern for others helps to divert anxiety about the seriousness of one's own damage.

There are also differences in the sense of conscious responsibility in an accident and in a disaster. The accident victim (for instance, in an automobile collision) is apt to have some manifest grounds for blaming himself. Since this is very painful, he is likely to defend himself by projection of blame onto others. This contributes to his feeling on bad terms with the world, irascible and irritable. In a disaster, one is relieved of this feeling of possibly being directly responsible for the event. There is a sense of something great and overwhelming, beyond the individual's control which on the conscious level has a relieving and exonerating effect. However, I do not think it eliminates more deep-lying and irrational feelings of culpability, the tendency to take what has befallen one as a punishment, of which I have already spoken repeatedly (cf. Schmideberg's observations on reactions to bombing as punishment[144]). This sense of having undergone a severe punishment contributes, as I have suggested, to the disaster victim's docility and need to be good. In the situation where he is surrounded by other victims, he has the opportunity for exercising the goodness to which he feels moved. This further motivates the altruistic reaction: take care of the others first. The depressed state of the disaster victim, his reduced self-esteem because of the damage he has suffered, contributes to his inclination to expect little for himself, his touching gratitude that anything should be done for him.

The main circumstances which distinguish the disaster victim from the accident victim would then appear to be: a sense of restoration of a world that seemed lost, less crucial conscious guilt, more opportunity for expiation (of unconscious guilt) through goodness, more possibility for diversion of concern for oneself to others, the possibility of feeling less damaged by comparison with others, and less grievance against the rest of the world for being unaffected.

Observers (and I think also disaster researchers) have tended to regard the disaster syndrome as a reassuring phenomenon. The description of disaster victims as "stunned" and "dazed" is often accompanied by remarks like: there was no hysteria, no panic, no wild excitement. One gets the impression that the observer expected more uncontrolled behavior and emotional expression, and was relieved to find the victims so quiet and well behaved. However, if the present reconstruction of the internal state of the person who appears stunned and dazed is approximately correct, we can see that this is a condition of severe suffering. Perhaps in

America particularly, where emotional control is highly valued, and the possibility of experiencing depression or despair
tends to be denied, the distress of the disaster victim, who
behaves with such satisfactory outward restraint, is likely
to be underestimated.

5.
Panic

Panic is a frequently anticipated but rarely occurring reaction to disaster.[145] I have discussed in the previous part the terrible fascination of the image of panic as an animal-like stampede in which wildly excited people crush each other to death. It would seem that the readiness to anticipate panic is more related to the haunting quality of this image than to observations of how people actually behave in danger situations.

While the image of the mad mob is probably of special importance because of its emotional significance, the term "panic" has a number of other meanings which it may be clarifying to distinguish:[146]

1. Intense subjective terror, with or without external justification.

2. Behavior of a non-useful or self-destructive sort motivated by extreme alarm (as when someone jumps from a high window of a house on fire just before the fire ladder reaches him).

3. "Contagion" of alarm in a group: the signs of others fear increases each individual's apprehensions.

4. Precipitate flight of a group of people from a danger which rightly or wrongly appears to be impossible to combat.

5. A group situation in which each individual's concern for his own threatened safety excludes regard for others.

6. A group situation where in the effort to flee from imminent danger individuals damage or destroy each other.

The term "panic" is also used for a combination of some or all of these phenomena. Since definitions are sometimes confused with empirical statements, a definition of "panic" which includes all the items listed may be taken as implying the mutual involvement of these phenomena in actuality. For this reason it seems useful to point out the extent to which some of these phenomena may occur independently of others. Precipitate flight may be the most useful action in certain situations (as, for instance, from a fire which one is unequipped to combat) and may not exclude regard for others. Even where each individual is so preoccupied with his own threatened safety that he can think of no one else, there may be no mutual damage among those who are fleeing together.[147] Thus the definition of "panic" as irrational and anti-social mass flight (i.e., as including items 2, 4, and 6) should not lead us to infer that every instance of precipitate group flight (4) is unuseful (2) or involves mutual damage among the fugitives (6).

Let us consider under what conditions a group of people trying to escape from imminent, extreme danger inflict damage on one another. We may take the following two instances as illustrative. In the Cocoanut Grove fire, a large crowd struggling to escape from the flames pushed desperately towards an exit which was blocked and people were crushed to death in the mass surge. Following the bombing of Hiroshima, a large crowd of survivors had taken refuge in a park beside a river, where they began to be threatened by fire spreading through the trees and bushes. "The frightened people in the park pressed closer and closer to the river, and finally the mob began to force some of the unfortunates who were on the very bank into the water," where they were drowned.[148] The common feature of such situations is that the escape route is partially or totally blocked at the same time that the way to safety seems so close at hand. Access to

space into which to escape is sharply restricted; it is inadequate to the numbers of people competing for it. The bodies
of others become obstacles interposed between the fugitive
and what he feels to be the only way out of an overpowering danger situation. It is under such conditions that people
may crush, trample or push others out of the way in their
struggle towards safety.

In general being trapped, finding oneself in an extreme
danger situation from which escape routes are blocked or
about to be cut off, rouses intense terror and is apt to set off
precipitate flight. Where there seems to be a danger of being
trapped, the fear of being caught in such a predicament may
drastically impair judgment; the individual's only thought
is to get out of the closing trap and he is unable to see into
what his flight precipitates him. Thus seamen on a burning
ship have sometimes jumped into water covered with flaming
oil and burned to death. A situation of real or imagined
entrapment thus seems to be the most likely to induce
destructive or self-destructive behavior.[149]

Many disaster situations (such as those in a bombed or
tornado-stricken city), while they may rouse subjective terror
in some individuals, do not usually lead to non-useful behavior, or precipitate flight, or loss of regard for others, or
mutual destructiveness among those endangered. Contagion
of alarm may occur in a threatened group. But it seems that,
perhaps more often, it is those who are calm and confident
who exercise the most influence on those around them.[150]

Since panic in the most terrible sense of mad, mutually
destructive mob flight so rarely occurs, but continues to be
so often anticipated, I should like to suggest what may be
some of the underlying fantasies which make this image such
a haunting one. If disaster comes, and many must die, the
more or less explicit thought of each individual is: rather
them than me. The individual pictures himself competing
with others for scarce chances of survival. Situations from
earlier life may be evoked in which the individual was one
of a crowd clamoring for a special favor, as children, for
instance, pressing towards mother each demanding the biggest

piece of cake. In the more extreme situation the crowd of desperate competitors is pictured each struggling to obtain the favors of fate which are not sufficient for all. A situation where life cannot be granted to all suggests that others would like to rob one of one's chance, just as one would be ready to sacrifice them in order to survive. There is a basic fantasy to the effect that the death of one person may assure the life of another (as if the gods required a sacrifice and would be appeased by the blood of the victims so that others would be allowed to live). Hence the image arises of a violent struggle for life in a crowd where each would kill the other in order to survive. Further, the idea of being subjected to the ruthless impact of other bodies in an agitated mass is not only frightening, but also gratifying. Intense excitement and particularly sado-masochistic satisfactions may be anticipated from such an experience. The fantasy of dying engulfed in a sea of bodies may evoke ectasy as well as terror.

Perhaps the myth from which the word "panic" comes may also give us a clue to a recurrent situation which underlies the fantasy of panic. It is told that the god Pan loved to sleep in the woods and resented being disturbed. He would revenge himself on those who interrupted his sleep by a sudden loud shout which made the hair bristle on their heads.[151] This was the original "panic" fear. Myths, like other major fantasies, are apt to present under a disguise important experiences of early childhood. The myth of Pan gives us the elements of disturbed sleep, anger, frightening noise, and extreme terror. I would suggest that an early childhood situation which contains the same elements is that of what Freud has called the "primal scene," that is, the intercourse of the parents as seen or overheard by the child. In this situation it is the child who is frightened when his sleep is disturbed by the parents' love-making. In the myth there is a reversal: it is the sleeper who frightens those who disturb his sleep. The primal scene contains many of the elements of the scene of panic. There is the impact of body on body, the mutual damage being read in by the bewildered child who mistakes the act for one of sadistic violence. There is the transformation of loving, protective beings into mad, animal-like creatures. This is the discrepancy which the child feels between the daytime and the nighttime parents. And the unbearable fright is what the child feels at seeing his parents so strangely transformed and withdrawn from him, as well as at the destructive implications of the act as he misunderstands it. The image of the primal scene may find a disguised counterpart in the image of panic, and may contribute to the terrifying fascination of the latter image.

Since our mastery of reality proceeds not only by the acquisition of information but also by the reduction of interfering fantasies, it seems relevant to take into consideration not only the rarity of real panic in the sense of mad mob flight, but also what may be some of the underlying fantasies which contribute to the frequency of the anticipation of such panic as a consequence of disaster.

6.
Egoism and altruism

ΛΛΛΛΛΛΛΛΛΛΛΛΛΛΛΛΛΛΛΛΛΛΛΛ

THOSE WHO HAVE UNDERGONE a disaster are apt to emerge from its impact with powerful feelings of love for their fellow men. "The general impression of observers is that injured and uninjured alike were more concerned for others than for themselves. . . . Each person became a saint for about ten days."[152] As one woman described her feelings after surviving a tornado: "It seemed that when you met anyone that had life in 'em, black or white, you just wanted to grab 'em and love 'em."[153] An adolescent girl, following the same experience, said: "Everytime you saw anybody you just hugged them. . . . Even your best enemies (sic) were your good friends now."[154]

There are probably many factors which contribute to this reaction. In the moment of extreme danger, which has preceded the appearance of this sentiment, there is apt to be a sharp constriction of feelings: one only cares about oneself, or oneself together with those who are closest and best loved. As one woman puts it, while she and her husband and children huddled together and a tornado blew away the house from over their heads: "We started prayin' if we could just come through alive, well, that's all we were askin' for. I said I felt it was rather selfish after it was all over. We were just sayin', 'God, please save us'—when we really meant, 'save everybody.' "[155] Another woman, alone with her daughter in the same predicament, tells the girl they had better pray: "And she (the daughter) said, 'Mother, I'm prayin' for Daddy.' And I said, 'Mary, I feel sure that Daddy's safe. Let's pray for the Lord to give us strength and courage to endure this.' "[156] Such concentration on oneself and those who are with one is facilitated by the illusion of centrality which we discussed earlier. The threatened persons imagine that the danger is exclusively focused on themselves. Afterwards, however, there is a feeling of compunction for the "selfishness" which was dominant in the moment of impact. So many others have suffered and one could not even spare a prayer for them. The impulse of generosity which follows is in part an effort at restitution for one's own abandonment of others immediately before. This is further reenforced by the need to be good, which we have noted already, as a reaction to the feeling of having undergone a severe punishment. One becomes more than usually sensitive to one's sins of "selfishness" and eager to atone for them.

In circumstances, even apart from a large scale disaster, where one has felt extreme anxiety about oneself or a beloved person (say, because of a serious illness), when the danger is past, there is apt to be a reaction to the intense constriction of feelings which the emergency has enforced. In the relief of escape from danger, the affections which had been focused defensively on the threatened object are released. There is a feeling of happy expansion as one's emotions are liberated and can turn towards the world at large. These positive feelings for others have the more vivacity following a phase of suspension. To make a comparison with a less drastic situation, the student who has been looking at nothing but his books during a siege of pre-examination study may, in a somewhat similar way, once his examinations are over, find the world of nature shining in a particularly fresh and vivid light.

Good feelings for others are moderated, in ordinary times, by negative feelings in varying degrees. I speak now not of specific, personal dislikes or ambivalence, but of a reservoir of negative feelings, deriving from a variety of frustrations and annoyances, which interfere with our feeling kindly to those around us. Under the shadow of a danger which threatens severe frustration, aggressive feelings are apt to become intensified (though they are also likely to be held in check under the pressure of anxiety). Once the danger is past, the aggressive feelings which the threat provoked become dissipated. The reservoir of negative feelings which contribute to everyday annoyance with others is at low ebb. There is the familiar exclamation of the person who has emerged successfully from an ordeal: "I don't hate anyone!"

These reactions to escape from danger, of expansion of affections and reduction of hostility, are common, as I have said, to situations other than large scale disasters. In the latter these responses are apt to be further intensified. For the world to which one turns with so much more positive and unmixed feelings than usual is a world that seemed lost and is now found again. So a woman whom I have quoted before describes her emergence from her ruined house after a tornado when she saw the whole neighborhood destroyed and thought she was the sole survivor: "It seemed like a strange place, another world. I felt like I was all alone. It was the loneliest feeling in the world." As she walks down the street she then sees other people coming out from under the ruins of their houses: "Finally that man raised up. And just about that time all five of those children raised up, and there wasn't a scratch on any of them." She is "almost hysterical" as she calls out to these fellow survivors. And she quickly becomes very active in helping others to find shelter or get to the hospital. Unaware that she is limping from an injury to her leg, she feels "like a million dollars."[157]

A disaster also sharply reduces the negative component in ambivalent feelings towards others. Whatever hostile wishes one may harbor receive unusual vicarious satisfaction from the disastrous event. As the negative component of one's ambivalence is thus satiated, it becomes temporarily quiescent and positive feelings become dominant. In relation to beloved persons the threat of the danger situation evokes the prospect of severe damage to them, something which has been at times unconsciously wished, but which when it seems about to materialize arouses great horror and alarm. These feelings are then followed by relief and intensified love when the danger has passed without the worst having happened.

When danger threatens persons who are objects of ambivalent feelings, there is apt to be a fear of what I would call one's "negative omnipotence." That is, one fears that one's worst wishes may come true, as if mocking gods were to take one's angry thoughts too literally. A woman, whom I cited earlier, who spoke of her terrible feelings of "insecurity" during the impact of the tornado, was mainly preoccupied with what might happen to her mother and sister in another part of the town. She remarked how in such a situation of danger and uncertainty, "You don't feel secure anywhere, with anybody or anything." And she added: "I always say insanity is my biggest fear. So always when I have anything happen to me that gives me this insecure feeling, I always think, 'Well, maybe this is before you go insane.' "[158] I would suggest that here there is an alarm that unconscious hostile wishes (towards mother and sister) are about to come true. But this would mean the loss of persons who are also loved and needed, and at the same time a loss of faith in one's own good impulses. The world seems about to yield to one's own worst wishes: badness within and without threatens to assume the ascendancy. The sense of loss of control of bad impulses and loss of protection of good objects (within and without) is expressed in the feeling: this is madness.

There follows the urgent need to assure oneself that the worst has not happened. This woman who was in such desperate anxiety about her mother and sister tells how she rushed to them immediately after the tornado had passed: "I jumped out of the car (blocked from going further by debris on the road) and just flew. I fell down three or four times before I got there. And I was just so scared that I guess it didn't make much difference whether wires were down or not. But fortunately we didn't have any current. . . . Finally

I could see my mother and sister coming this way and they were calling to me and I was calling to them as loud as I could. So we all experienced the same feeling and we couldn't really believe that we were seeing each other until we actually felt each other."[159] Past ambivalence contributes to such intensity of positive feelings towards loved ones who had been imagined lost, and also perhaps in this case to self-punishment (in falling down and exposure to the danger of fallen wires). Also the imagined loss of loved persons evokes the realization of how much one needs them, which is apt to be latent in everyday life.

Because of the unconscious belief in the omnipotence of thoughts, disaster victims are apt to suppress or repress the fantasies of fatality to loved ones which may have beset them in the moment of danger. Thus we have heard how a man who was away from his family when a tornado struck said that he "expected the worst," but quickly followed this with "I didn't give it too much thought," and the assertion that he was exclusively preoccupied with the problem of getting home.[160] In the following instance we find, however, a very explicit fantasy about the death of a loved one, which became so vivid that the person imagined dead was at first not recognized when he appeared quite undamaged. The situation was one where an upstairs back porch, on which a number of people were sitting, suddenly collapsed. A large party of relatives inside the house started rushing downstairs and towards the back of the building to find out what had happened and who had been hurt. One woman describes her thoughts during these moments of uncertainty: "I was thinking about being left a widow. Somehow, I just knew my husband had been killed. . . I remember while I was running around to the back trying to get used to the fact of being a widow and what it would be like. . . I think it's that that kept me from seeing my husband when I got out in back. He was right in plain sight. But I was so sure that he had been killed that . . . I just couldn't recognize him. . . You get the worst possible picture in your mind and you can't think of anything else. . . I just sort of saw my husband lying out there

mangled or crushed. . . I kept looking at the porch trying
to find him. I don't know why I didn't look any place else,
because he was right out there in plain sight."[161] Such anticipations of the worst are in part motivated by the wish to
defend oneself against an overwhelming shock; as this woman
says she was trying to get used to the idea of being a widow.
However, her vivid conviction that her husband was mangled and dead most probably drew some of its force from
the negative component of ambivalent feelings.

I should like to digress for a moment here to remark on
what appear to be cultural differences in respect to the tendencies just described. The large family party which was
tragically interrupted by the porch collapse was that of a
Jewish family. The woman who so quickly pictures her husband dead was not alone in having this reaction. Studies of
traditional Jewish culture have shown that in these families
apprehensions about damage and death to family members
are very frequent on the conscious level.[162] If husband or
child fails to wear his warm coat, for instance, the mother
readily expresses alarm that they will have got a chill, from
which will follow pneumonia, from which they will die. In
Protestant American culture there is not this readiness for
alarm in everyday life. Whether there is less ambivalence
towards family members we do not know. What we can say
is that there are different defenses against such ambivalence,
which appear, for instance, in the tendency to suppress and
repress fantasies of fatality to loved ones which may be stimulated by a disaster.

One of the most frequent types of false rumor following a
disaster is that of the death of particular persons.[163] As a
consequence, for days afterwards people in the disaster-
stricken community keep running into acquaintances whom
they had supposed dead. A tornado victim relates, in telling
about the feelings of good will among the townspeople after
the disaster: "I met this lady and she said, 'Mrs. Miller, I'm
glad to see you. The very first person that we heard was killed
was you.' "[164] Here again we may suppose that the negative
sector of ambivalent feelings towards neighbors and acquaint-

ances has been satisfied by their supposed destruction so
that positive feelings then become predominant. Even where
acquaintances have not been rumored to be dead, the fact
that they have suffered injuries or loss of relatives or property has a similar emotional effect.

The concern for others as well as, or more than oneself
which disaster victims sometimes feel in the moment of impact may be in part derived from the need to be good to
escape the threatening punishment. The woman who said
she had felt selfish afterwards because she had not prayed
for others quickly excused herself with saying that of course
she was thinking of her children. That is, she was praying
for them and wanted herself to survive for their sake. Thus
she was altruistic, though on a smaller scale than she later
thought she should have been.[165] Another mother tells the
interviewer: "When the storm hit ... I just prayed to the
good Lord to bring me through and let me see my kids alive
and well." The interviewer rephrases this: "I see, you were
thinking of your children." The woman then replies: "I
certainly were, and the thought of myself never entered."[166]
What the woman had at first said was that she prayed for
both herself and her children. The interviewer, by acknowledging only her concern for her children, succeeds in acti-
vating the feeling of guilt that one has thought of oneself at
all (perhaps because at that moment one had thought of one-
self·above all), so that she quickly affirms that "the thought of
myself never entered." If in the moment of extreme danger
the feeling occurs that the loss of loved ones would be less
unbearable than the loss of one's own life, there is apt to be
shame and guilt for such feelings afterwards. They are suppressed or repressed, and expiated by increased love.

Some who in the moment of extreme danger do think of
others rather than themselves may be helped in this by a
conviction of their own invulnerability. If damage is done,
they assume it will be to others and not to themselves. Thus
a woman relates that she was once in a car with friends at
night on an icy highway when the car went into a bad skid.
In the moment of anticipating a serious smash-up this woman

thought: "If the Smiths (her fellow-passengers in the car) are killed, I'll adopt their children." In this fantasy she took for granted her own survival. Such confidence in one's own invulnerability facilitates regard for others in an emergency. It is also true that the person who has firm positive attachments to others is less subject to anxiety about himself.

In anticipation of the outcome of a disaster, the image of oneself as helping others afterwards also may serve to blot out the picture of oneself as reduced to helplessness or beyond help. A bus driver in Worcester tells about his feelings while his bus was being overturned by the tornado: "I thought it was the end of all of us. . . At one point I imagined leavin' my family an' I could even imagine the funeral they were holdin' for me. . . But the thoughts were always in my mind of holding on and bein' able to stand up an' get out of there an' help. . . I can't ever remember stop thinking of what to do after." The thoughts of what he would do to help the injured passengers for whom he felt responsible apparently pushed aside the apprehension of his own death.

The feeling of helplessness, which is present at least during the time that one is undergoing the impact of an overpowering force, can be mastered afterwards by helping others. One then has the feeling: it is they and not I who are helpless. Similarly, by focusing attention on others' injuries one can put off awareness of one's own. This same bus driver worked valiantly to extricate injured passengers from the damaged bus. During this time he was able to ward off alarm about his own injuries. "I lost part of my thumb and it was hanging from the end. An' the thing that was making me the most impatient of it all was trying to get that piece of thumb outa people's faces as I was workin' on them. An' I kept trying to bite it off an' feelin' if I could only remove it. It kept botherin' me so much. An' a little thing like that after the great tragedy that had just struck! It seems funny now that those things you remember so clearly." Apparently while he was absorbed in rescue work, his feelings about his severed thumb were not those appropriate to a frightening injury, but rather a sense of impatience and bother. His wish to bite off the dangling piece of thumb may have expressed a number of motives: it's not something I need, not a terrible loss, it's only in the way; or, it's just like a bit of torn finger nail that one could bite off. There may also have been an effort to transform passivity into activity: it was not cut off me, I sever it myself. In any case the sequel suggests that during this time he was repressing his more serious feelings about this injury. After he had brought the injured bus passengers to the hospital and confided them to the care of doctors and nurses, explaining the injuries of one and another, a nurse came up to him, "an' she took me by the thumb an' —this is the part that I'm almost ashamed to relate—that when she took me by the thumb I keeled over, an' evidently I landed on the floor down there."[167] Thus when the moment came when he could no longer displace his concern to others' injuries but was forced to face his own, the terror which threatened him had to be warded off by loss of consciousness.

We may distinguish two dynamic patterns in this connection. An individual may be sufficiently concerned for others, because of strong emotional ties or sense of responsibility, that as a consequence his concern for himself is reduced. Or an individual may be impelled to displace onto others concern about himself which is fraught with too much anxiety. In other words reduced anxiety about oneself may be a *consequence* of concern for others, or the need to escape too great anxiety about oneself may be a *motive* for concentrating attention on others. In making this distinction I do not mean to exclude the possibility of both factors working together. The individual who has strong attachments and a sense of responsibility for others may also utilize these defensively to reduce alarm about his own fate. He can avoid falling into the position of a helpless child by seeing others in this role and himself in that of a strong parent: it is they who are weak and I who am strong. And similarly in respect to physical damage: it is they who are injured—I am intact. It would seem that where this position is predominantly defensive (I care for the others in order not to be alarmed about myself), there is more apt to be a belated breakthrough of extreme anxiety about onself. This occurs, as in the case of the bus driver, when the situation no longer justifies the displacement to others.

It has been often said that extreme situations bring out the best and worst in people. We have seen some of the ways in which a disaster situation stimulates generous feelings and behavior. We may observe that there are times when the opposite occurs. Where the situation is one in which there is a competition for the means of survival, acts of extreme brutality may occur. So following the sinking of the Titanic, some of the survivors in the lifeboats felt threatened by those who were swimming towards them hoping to climb into the boats; perhaps the boats would capsize or sink— there did not seem to be room for more. "Some boats beat off the freezing victims; fear-crazed men and women struck with oars at the heads of swimmers."[168] In the shipwreck of the Medusa (the French ship bound for Africa which foundered on a reef in 1816, and whose dying survivors on their raft are commemorated in the painting of Géricault), desperate people, crowded together on an ill-built raft, drifting under a tropic sun, pushed their dying shipmates into the water so that they should not deplete the dwindling supply of wine. And, as starvation threatened the ever lessening number of survivors, they looked longingly at the bodies of the dead, and ended by eating them.[169]

It is only under special conditions that the drastic alternative is really presented of having to sacrifice others in order to survive. Such situations occur much more often in fantasy than in reality. I have discussed this in connection with anticipations of panic, in speaking of the emotional predicament of the person whose loved ones are in danger while he is not, and in relation to the thoughts of endangered persons who implicitly hope that others and not themselves will be the victims. Often this sacrifice of others for one's own survival remains on the level of fantasy. Then there is only the guilt for egoistic thoughts, which impels the individual to make good in subsequent altruistic actions.

Another kind of anti-social behavior which may occur in

the disorder created by a disaster is looting. Evidently this is facilitated by the interruption of police supervision. But it would seem also that in some persons there is a shift in moral attitudes, produced by the disaster, which makes them feel justified in doing things which they would not do otherwise. Adhering to moral rules may require to some extent a familiar environment. Where this is no longer present there may be a feeling of exemption from restraints. So, for instance, some people allow themselves certain indulgences abroad which they would not feel right about at home. When a familiar setting has been destroyed by a disaster, some persons may experience a similar sense of suspension of usual restrictions.

The occurrence of a disaster also carries the significance for some individuals that the authorities, human or supernatural, are unable to keep destructive forces under control. Perhaps such feelings are more easily stimulated in the case of man-made destruction, such as bombing, where also there is the demand that home authorities protect their subjects against its rigors. As the authorities fail to prevent the destruction from going on, there may be the feeling that the individual is absolved from controlling his own lower impulses: immoral authorities cannot expect to inspire moral behavior in their subjects.[170] Even in natural disasters, there may be the feeling that supernatural authorities have violated their contract with man to treat him well if he behaves well. With the breaking of this contract, men are freed to do as they please.

The destructive force which rages in a disaster may afford a vicarious gratification to the destructive impulses of those who witness it as well as a stimulus to the unleashing of impulses ordinarily held in check. The following account of incidents during the great Chicago fire (a description which may be somewhat exaggerated for literary effect) illustrates the combination of illicit acts, in pillaging, and delight in the spectacle of destruction. "The people were mad. Men on all sides were to be seen frenzied with drink. They smashed windows, reckless of the severe wounds inflicted on their

hands, fighting viciously for the spoils ... Women, hollow-
eyed and brazen-faced ... moved here and there, stealing,
scolding shrilly, and laughing with one another at some particularly 'splendid' gush of flame or 'beautiful' falling-in of
a roof."[171] Much heavy drinking went on during the Chicago
fire, according to reports, liquor supplies of saloons and ware-
houses being raided by "rough, transient fellows," while
some of the rich as well engaged in "bacchanalian revels."[172]
Apart from the suspension of social supervision, there are
probably a number of subjective factors which are conducive
to such orgies in extreme situations. Besides the feeling that
the powers have shown themselves to be bad or weak and
the stimulating example of destructive forces unleashed, there
may be an impulse to defend oneself against the fear of being
deprived and abandoned by fulsome indulgence. Thus im-
bibing freely, for instance, may serve to ward off the fear of
loss of needed supplies which the disaster seems to threaten.
The reminder of the imminence of death impels one to
consume all one can while there is still time. Absorption in
enjoyment and a sense of exuberant vitality may then in turn
make death seem remote and unreal.

Such orgiastic reactions contrast with the chastened behavior of those who in response to disaster become more noble
and self-sacrificing. There would seem to be in the two cases
opposite feelings about the individual's relations to the powers that be. For those who react with increased goodness, the
disaster may have been experienced as a punishment reminding them of unfulfilled moral demands, which they then
strive to realize to ward off further punishment and to regain
the love and protection of the powers. Those who, on the other
hand, react with reduced moral restraint and increased self-
indulgence seem to have become disillusioned with the powers: it seems futile to try to win their favors, and one had
better grasp whatever gratification one can for oneself. Or
it may seem that any moral powers have suspended operations, abandoning the world to the sway of brute force. There
is no longer any superior agency that the individual need
make an effort to placate. There would also seem to be a

different relation to one's own destructive impulses in each case. Those who participate in the destructive effects of a disaster are glad to find a precedent for letting go. Those who are impelled, on the other hand, to restitutive activities feel alarmed at the prospect of their latent hostile wishes being realized.

We may note that in wartime Britain and in recent peace-time disasters in the United States the incidence of anti-social behavior in the form of looting, for instance, was slight. On the other hand, increase in good will and kindly behavior towards others was widespread.[173] As in the case of anticipations of panic and madness, so here with other deviant behavior, the apprehension that disaster may unleash a great surge of what is worst in human nature is little confirmed by actual events.

7.
Activity and emotion

A DANGER SITUATION carries the threat not only of damage and loss but of an overwhelming anxiety, which may be equally feared. Anxiety is a feeling which it is often difficult to keep within bounds. In the early phases of life, the infant organism may be flooded with anxiety under the pressure of unsatisfied needs with which it is helpless to cope. The usual reaction of the infant is one of diffuse emotional expression, crying and thrashing about. For the infant, this is apt to have the useful result of summoning the mother, who can relieve his distress. In normal maturation, with the acquisition of the capacity for foresight and for independent activity, anxiety increasingly assumes a signal function. That is, it is released in moderate amounts as a warning of oncoming danger, and serves to set off various adaptive actions so that overwhelming distress may be avoided.[174]

Different modes of upbringing contribute to different ways of managing anxiety. To acknowledge or even to feel fear may be regarded as shameful. The persistence of the tendency to appeal for help by emotional expression may be encouraged or disparaged. Individual self-sufficiency may be more or less of a value. Belief in the possibility of effective action may be weak or strong. Differences of upbringing in these matters make for individual differences in emotion and action in extreme situations.

In different cultures also different values may be commonly assigned to the control of fear, emotional expressiveness or restraint, independence or demands for help. Thus, for instance, in a recent study of cultural differences in reaction to pain, it appears that among Italians and Jews the sufferer is expected to express his distress freely, to cry out for help quite literally. Rather than appearing shameful, helplessness evokes positive responses of intensified love and care. In individuals of old American families, on the other hand, there is a firm restraint on emotional expression and a concentration on what can be done. In hospitals staffed with American personnel, it is often felt that the Italian and Jewish patients "exaggerate" their suffering with their crying and complaints. The old American appears as the "good patient" who is properly cooperative; he reports on his symptoms like a detached observer, assuming the role of a member of the team, together with doctors and nurses, who will work on his case. Italian and Jewish patients felt distressed at being taken to the hospital, where they were deprived of the familial environment sensitively responsive to their expressions of suffering. For American patients getting to the hospital was more apt to be reassuring: here the maximum facilities were available, and now things would really get done.[175]

The limited material available on cultural differences in disaster situations suggests comparable variations in emotional expressiveness. In the incident of the porch collapse where the persons involved were Jewish, the preponderance of intense emotional expression precluded useful action. The people who rushed out of the house to find some of their relatives fallen to the ground, others clinging perilously to the half-fallen porch and crying for help, were too distraught to do anything but scream and mill around. Help had to be brought and summoned by outsiders, alerted by the uproar. As one woman in the group affected by the disaster describes it: "It was like a panic . . . everybody was screaming and running just as fast as they could to get out there and see what happened . . . They were milling around like a herd of cattle. Nobody was doing anything but screaming and trying to find their loved ones." A neighbor reports similarly, "They were all gathered around there shouting at the top of their lungs. I thought the world was coming to an end or something like that. I never heard anything like it in all my life." This expression of distress continued among those who accompanied the injured to the hospital afterwards: "The people at the hospital were cutting up worse then than they did at the accident. There was more screaming going on than I ever heard before. It sounded more like a nuthouse than a hospital . . . The nurses kept trying to quiet everybody down, but they just kept on screaming."[176] Subsequently there were complaints about the inadequate care given by the hospital staff, which would seem in part related to their unresponsiveness to this clamorous emotional distress, and probably their disapproval of it.

Similar emotional manifestations have been observed among Italians. In a village shaken by an earthquake, "Shouts, wailings, imprecations, desperate cries of terror and of appeal to the saints resounded from all quarters of the town. The still night suddenly became one of indescribable uproar."[177]

In contrast to this, there are other cultures, among them the American, in which a high value is placed on emotional restraint and where giving way to excited expressions of alarm and distress is regarded as more or less disgraceful. In American child rearing, the child's tendency to use his muscular resources for uncoordinated emotional expression (in crying or fits of rage) is strongly discouraged, while his potentialities for organized motor acts which enable him to get somewhere and do something are fostered and rewarded. In current American child training literature, the major motive of the small child is said to be that of wanting to explore his world.[178] Thus potentialities for mastering the environment by moving through space and manipulating things are stressed, while those for emotional expressiveness tend to be played down. Similarly independent activity is favored rather than appeals for help. Excitement, alarm, clamorous expression of emotion, distress which reduces the capacity for efficient action are all disapproved, while positive value attaches to keeping cool and getting things done.

Americans who have been involved in disasters repeatedly stress the importance of keeping calm and express pride in having kept calm themselves. Few describe themselves as having been emotionally distraught, though they may speak of others in this way.[179] Among college students who escaped from a burning dormitory, "The most frequent answer of informants to the question, 'Do you think other people were acting rationally after they got out of the dorm?' was 'No.' To the question, 'Do you think your own actions were rational and logical?' every informant answered, 'yes.' "[180] A man reports with apparent pride of his family who had just weathered a tornado: "All of us were cut and bruised, but no one let out a yelp or anything."[181] Relating her experience during a tornado, a woman says, "The other two ladies (whom she was with) were fairly frightened, but for some reason I never was really frightened." And she tells how her adolescent son, a boy scout prepared for emergencies, was busy at school during the disaster, "trying to help keep the others calm who weren't so calm and didn't have the training and instruction that he had."[182]

High demands are made on oneself to remain calm even in very moving circumstances. The woman who had thought she was the sole survivor of the tornado tells how she first saw others rising up out of the ruins of their houses: "And finally that man raised up and I—I almost got hysterical. I said, 'Are you all right?' And on the last word I kind of raised my voice. And I thought, 'Well now, I can't do this. I've got to be calm.' " The same woman, speaking of a subsequent severe storm during which she felt no fear, says, "I still think that old calm feeling is the best thing you can have."[183]

Mothers may take the occasion of such extreme happenings to continue their children's education in emotional control. A mother tells of having been separated from her children during the tornado, she being at home and they at school. Having hastened to the school she finds her fourteen-year-old daughter, and "she was crying up just a storm. And I said, 'Well, just a minute, Sally. Where's Billy and Grady (the two other children who were also at school)?' 'Mother, they're all right.' I said, 'Well, what in the world are you crying for then if you're all right?' I said, 'Shut up your crying.' ... The thing of it was they were afraid I had been killed, and that's why she was crying. She said, 'Mother, we didn't know what had happened to you.' And I said, 'Well, I'm all right now and let's just hush crying.' " This woman describes herself as having been "just as calm as a cucumber." And later in speaking about her children, apparently forgetting about her daughter's crying fit, and bringing the picture of their behavior into accordance with her ideal, she says, "They took it mighty calm. They sure did."[184]

Painful emotions, such as that of overwhelming alarm, thus seem to be successfully warded off in such individuals by "that old calm feeling." Or, at least, this is the version of their experience which they prefer to give, the model to which they strive to conform. What is more, emotions which in some other cultures would be considered both permissible and not wholly unpleasant are equally interfered with. The upsurge of feelings of a person who had thought himself alone in a ruined world when he finds others still alive is quickly countered by the self-admonition to keep calm. A child who finds again the mother she feared killed is told to stop her crying at once. We may perhaps discern here a general attitude towards emotions which extends beyond situations where distress may impede useful action. A negative value is apt to be placed on any emotion which has an admixture of pain. Only purely euphoric feelings are fully accepted. On the other hand, spontaneity is also highly valued. But it is difficult to maintain it where one must interfere with negative and mixed feelings. The ideal of euphoric feelings which are both continuous and spontaneous is hard to achieve. We shall see in the next chapter the valiant efforts which are made in the time following a disaster to maintain this ideal of euphoric feelings despite all damage and deprivation.

The insight that children will not be overwhelmed by alarm if their parents are unfrightened comes easily to American parents since they are already so strongly disposed in favor of keeping calm. Parents try especially to keep calm in front of their children both in order to help them through the immediate situation and to give them an example of how one should behave. Children generally are favored objects for the projection of grown-ups' fears. One can avoid recognizing one's own fear by acknowledging it in another; assuaging it in the other, one at the same time reduces it in oneself. In relation to children, one is confirmed in one's adult status, kept mindful of one's greater capacities for both inner and outer control. One mother says, apropos of a recent threat of a tornado, when her children played in the cellar to which she had sent them and "didn't pay any attention" to the storm: "That's the thing I try not to do is show any fear in front of the children. And it will help you . . . because you know you've got to be calm around the children, why, it'll help you to be."[185] Another mother tells her teen-aged daughter, who is alarmed by the same threat of another tornado: "We just got to keep ourselves so we won't unnerve the little one."[186]

The idea of keeping calm is explicitly connected with the requirement of being able to be useful and helpful. If one becomes emotionally distraught one's capacity to help will be impaired. Conversely, if one concentrates on the work to be done, it helps one to maintain the desirable emotional control. One woman explains how in an emergency situation she tries to help others not to get upset: "I usually just talk with them and tell them that getting upset and all will just make bad matters worse. That if they will try to stay calm they can protect themselves more than if they get all upset— well, they can't protect theirselves nor help anyone else. I have found out I believe that if a person is trained to help the other fellow and to consider the other fellow that he won't let himself go so because he'll think, 'Well now, I might be needed.' " She tells how she applies this to her twelve-year-old daughter who has been frightened of a possible recurrence of the tornado. The mother has been "trying to sit down and reason with her and telling her that if there was to be something that she personally could do to help, if she allowed her emotions to run away with her, she won't be in any condition to do anything. So the first thing for her to learn is to keep herself under control and then she might render some aid in some way. But she certainly can't help anyone else as long as she needs aid herself."[187] Another mother relates how her son who is a boy scout "said what he thinks about is trying to keep hisself calm enough to where if something was to happen he would be in shape to try to help somebody who needs him. I think that's helped him more than anything. I think if he didn't have that to look forward to he would get more nervous." And she adds, speaking of the disaster victims who required medical aid for nervous upsets: "I think most of those who had to have medical aid to overcome it were perhaps those who sit down and considered themselves first and foremost. I think when you have others to consider you can throw off your own feelings better."[188]

Thus we find a benign circle in effect here. One remains calm in order to be in fit condition to be useful to others. And being useful in turn reduces emotional upset and nervousness. There is, as it were, a resolve to confine anxiety to a signal function, to exclude the energies stimulated by an extreme situation from channels of emotional elaboration and expression, and to direct them into useful activity. One of the things that contributes to this tendency is a strong dislike for being in a position of needing help, preferring to feel: it is others who need help, not I. We shall see this operative later on in the aversion to accepting what is felt to be charity in the period following a disaster. In the impact phase and immediately afterwards there is the feeling that if one becomes overwhelmed by emotional distress, one reverts to the infantile position of being helpless and needing to be taken care of by others, which is incompatible with self-esteem. We may relate this to a general American tendency to fear becoming dependent, which means a loss of adult status.[189] Keeping calm in order to be helpful rather than helpless is an ideal which evidently is not always achieved in practice. However, for those who share this ideal becoming distraught and inefficient in extreme situations entails the added distress of reduced self-esteem. Thus a woman reports about a high school girl, a schoolmate of her son, that having become "hysterical" during the tornado she was afterwards "ashamed of herself that she didn't stay calm enough."[190]

Confidence in know-how also helps in maintaining calm and efficiency. Such confidence is related to the general American emphasis on skills and belief that all problems can be solved by the discovery of proper techniques. One woman tells how as the tornado was coming on she was occupied with "discussing the facts of what we should do" with two neighbor women, bringing to bear the scout lore which she had picked up from her husband and son as to the most protected parts of the house in such an emergency. "We just felt that we would be protected if we used our heads sensibly." And in telling how her husband came through unscathed due to his quick-witted and correct behavior, she says: "He would have been killed if he hadn't used what brain he had ... if he hadn't used what training and information he had."[191] It seems likely that persons who attribute their survival in this way to their own competence are less susceptible to a subjective near-miss reaction than those who feel it was just luck that they were not killed. Those who feel that they have come through because of their cool application of know-how would seem to have escaped the most devastating experience of helplessness and feeling of being at the mercy of forces beyond their control. Of course we should keep in mind that these accounts of having remained calm and efficient throughout an extreme event may result from a certain amount of retrospective distortion. Temporary upset and reduction of effectiveness may be repressed or suppressed because such experiences are in themselves distressing and because they conflict with the individual's ideal image of himself.

Explicit formulations of the virtues and advantages of keeping calm are put forward particularly by disaster victims reflecting on their experience after a considerable lapse of time. The statements which I have been citing to this effect are drawn from interviews with people in San Angelo, Texas, who had survived a tornado which took a heavy toll of lives and property, who had rebuilt their houses, many of them adding storm cellars, and who a year later had been barely missed by another tornado. It was following the latter event that they expressed the views just quoted. In the year that had passed since the disaster they had had the problem of coping with anticipations of another tornado, feelings of alarm about any sign of stormy weather. They had struggled to master such apprehensiveness in themselves and their children, and in so doing were led to elaborate their view of ideal behavior in a danger situation. Also they had probably in the meanwhile revised their accounts of the disaster, playing down their feelings of distress at the time and embellishing the picture of themselves as calm and competent. Other disaster victims, interviewed within a briefer time of the event, expressed similar attitudes, only with less articulateness and elaboration. The common implicit values would seem to have become more conscious and more fully expressed when, as time passed, recurrent fears required a reenforcement of defenses against alarm. Then previously unverbalized attitudes were formulated for the purpose of "reasoning" with fearful children and with the fearfulness in oneself. It is my impression that these Texas tornado victims have thus, under the pressure of circumstances, formulated as an explicit doctrine certain attitudes which are widely shared in American culture but not so often put into words.

While the capacity to keep fear and other distressing emotions within limits facilitates doing useful work, it is equally true, as we have noted, that getting involved in some pressing activity is an effective defense against disturbing emotions. A woman who during a storm which threatened to precipitate a tornado kept bustling around the house trying to cope with the influx of torrential rain says: "You keep busy and not let fear overtake you."[192] The college boy mentioned previously, who on coming into a disaster-stricken town was appalled to find himself so close to death, speaks of "a little nervousness which I needed to forget by doing something." He acknowledges that he was at first "surprised" that there could be so much destruction and that something like that could come so close to him—"surprise" being here, we may suppose, an understatement for more painful feelings. Once he got busy helping to remove debris, he found such feelings diminishing. At the sight of dead and injured being carried out of the ruins, he says, "Well, I can't say that I had too strong a feeling about that . . . From the time that I began working, well, I guess after that not too much surprised me."[193]

Similarly a man who came back home to a tornado-stricken town, and, after ascertaining the safety of his own family, threw himself into rescue activities, stresses his absorption in these tasks and his lack of emotion throughout. "Just to be perfectly honest about it, I was so doggone busy I didn't pay too much attention to what was going on other than my own work with the group that I was in. In the group that I was in, why, they wasn't anybody out of sorts or upset or anything like that. They just said, 'Well, boys, we've got a job to do—let's do it. The worst has happened, or the worst is over with—now we have to clean it up.'" Here we can see the additional reassurance provided by feelings of solidarity with others involved in a common task, as well as the identification with the strong and active as a defense against identification with the victims. There is also the tendency to assimilate this exceptional and tragic task of uncovering the bodies of dead and injured to more ordinary work: a job to be done. Speaking about the dead and injured who were being carried out, this same man says, "You just didn't stop to see who they were—or at least I didn't. I was in this group of men and we were either going or coming or in digging and someone would say, 'Well, there goes so-and-so.' Well, you'd look and that would be all—they'd be taking them out." The sight of an injured man he knew "didn't excite me any. I knew he was hurt but as far as feeling on the inside—I didn't. It didn't affect me emotionally or any way like that."[194]

This man repeats over and over in his account of the disaster that he was not emotionally disturbed by it. One gets the impression of a very strong need to ward off intense or painful feelings. Such an individual may build up defenses against the emotions he fears, which may be of great usefulness in emergencies. This was the same man who, as distinguished from most of his fellow townsmen had taken the advance warnings of the tornado sufficiently seriously to plan with his wife exactly what should be done in case it came. Thus he was protecting himself against the danger of being taken by surprise, in which case he might have been overwhelmed by painful emotions. After the event, as we see, he found equally effective defenses against disturbing feelings in exhausting activity of a needed and useful kind. Thus there are certain defenses against affect which may make an individual very useful in an extreme situation. We may recall the bus driver whose efficient rescue activities were partly motivated by the need to scotomize his own injuries. Similarly the woman whom I have cited before, who spoke so much about the merits of "that old calm feeling," who when she heard herself raising her voice to hail other survivors quickly reminded herself to keep calm and so on, seems to have been very effective in helping others to get to shelter and to the hospital in the immediate post-disaster phase. The man whom I quoted just now, who was too "doggone busy" to feel anything, acknowledges that after a day or two he began to feel sorry for people who had suffered severe losses. Apparently in such instances the phase of affectlessness, insured by exhausting activity, allows for unconscious preparation for subsequent experience of painful feelings.

Having so much work to do following a disaster is sometimes explicitly welcomed as a means of warding off distressing feelings. As one woman puts it, "I felt that maybe if we didn't have all that work to do we could have set around and let ourselves think about it. And could be that it would have made us more nervous. But we didn't have time."[195] A woman whose mother was killed in a tornado speaks of how fortunate it was that there were so many practical problems to keep her busy immediately afterwards, occupation with which prevented the most intensely painful feelings about what had happened from emerging. "Losing our home and everything, losing your mother, would have been a terrible shock, but having so much to do along with the disaster —to find a place to live an' take care of the children an' get things cleaned up afterwards—it's just been really a good thing for us, if you know what I mean."[196] In this latter instance, submitting oneself to all the heavy tasks imposed by the disaster may also be a form of penance motivated by guilt feelings towards the dead.

The American tendency to prefer motor activity to the welling up of inner emotion is expressed in verbal formulations which translate feelings into motor terms. Thus, for instance, a college boy speaks of his reactions to uncovering a dead body: "I dug out a body with some of the boys up there and it kinda, kinda threw me. So I thought, well, I'd go—go home and get away from it."[197] We may suppose that there were here at least incipient feelings of horror and fear and the wish to efface terrifying and painful visions from one's memory. These are then expressed in terms of motor images and motor intents.

The urge to activity and eagerness to be useful on the part of rescue workers following a disaster does not necessarily lead to a high level of efficiency. Evidently it is often difficult to know what to do, facilities are lacking, and, despite the frequent disclaimers which we have noted, people are upset. It has been observed that people who come in from outside the impact area, and who have close ties to those who have just undergone danger and damage, tend to be hyperactive, to work themselves to the point of exhaustion in their anxiety to help, but to work at a low level of efficiency.[198] A doctor who was in the tornado-stricken area in Worcester describes in the following way a policeman who came into a badly damaged section: "He was overwhelmed by what he saw, as I interpret his behavior, and he just ran around . . . He was just running around and I don't know what he thought he was doing, that is, I don't know what he did. I'm sure he thought he was doing the best he could, but he didn't do anything."

The doctor describes his own efforts to be useful, in which he started out with the confident feeling that as a doctor he could be of special help and where he ended with a sense of frustration and futility. Coming first on a woman with a wounded arm, he looked around in the debris for something with which to make a tourniquet, and used for this purpose an electric iron cord with an iron permanently attached to it. As he reflected afterwards there were strips of material lying around which might have been more suitable, but somehow he took the unwieldy cord of the electric iron. He tells of his ineffective efforts to get dazed but uninjured survivors to help him to move injured persons. However, when someone joined him who wanted to help, he sent this would-be helper away to get bandages, and they failed to find each other again. Coming on a woman pinned down under the wreckage of her house, which he was unable to lift, he went off to try to get a jack from a car. He then became involved in trying to extricate a young man whose leg was caught in an overturned car, and so on. He moved from one group to another of the injured without being able to give effective aid. The feeling then overcame him that: "there was nothing you could do. And I felt frustrated and angry that I thought I could do something and it turned out I could do practically nothing." Thinking in retrospect about what he would have done differently if he had it to do over, he says, "I think I would do one thing at a time instead of trying to do so many at once. Christ knows there was a million things to do, that one can't be a god, unfortunately. I would take care of that first woman as completely as I could and then go on to the next one."[199]

Thus there appears to be in some rescuers the urge to undo

all the damage at once, as exemplified in this doctor's moving, as he judges afterwards, too rapidly through the devastated area, unable to content himself with giving limited, but perhaps more efficient help to those he first encounters. There is here both an ambition to take in one's scope the whole of the damage and make it good again (to be a god), and a great impatience to get things back as they should be.

Different individuals who participate in rescue work express different estimates of the efficiency of their work. Feelings of adequacy or inadequacy in such activities may be related to several factors besides that of the work actually accomplished. I have spoken of the functions of strenuous activity following a disaster as a defense against painful feelings. Such activities have both an alloplastic and an autoplastic purpose: there is the manifest wish to do something useful and the less conscious wish to escape from distress. A person's feeling that he was not able to do much may reflect his inability to ward off anxiety and depression by his activities which may have been from an external point of view more useful than he thinks. And conversely, a sense of satisfaction in what one did may indicate success in mastering painful feelings, which may accompany varying degrees of actual usefulness.

The longing to undo the damage may be more or less frustrated by a realization of irretrievable loss. Here evidently the nature of the damage or loss which each individual has suffered affects his feelings of adequacy or inadequacy to be useful after a disaster. A man whose father was killed in a tornado tells of his feelings of how little he could do to help survivors. His powerlessness to restore his father to life becomes symbolized by the hopelessness of trying to illuminate the darkness, to search for survivors under the debris, with the feeble little flashlight which was all he had. "It's an awful feeling, I'll tell you that right now. Just so many people there—you want to help them all and you can't help so many at once . . . Then just a little bitty flashlight—it ain't much of anything to look for anybody. But I just had a little old two-cell with me."[201] A young man expresses a similar feeling of helplessness after he and his friends had dug out of the wreckage the body of a boy they all knew. "So we just set around a minute. We didn't know just exactly what to do."[202] Thus activity may come to a standstill when one is forced to recognize damage which no effort can undo. However, as we have noted, on the part of those who are not personally affected by such loss, persistence in strenuous activity may serve to ward off any vivid awareness of the irretrievable.

Among some survivors of a disaster, as well as those who come to their aid, there is an exceptional output of energy in the time immediately following. "Every disaster produces stories of individuals who work for incredibly long periods of time without rest."[203] This is in part related to the urge to undo the damage as quickly as possible. So one woman describes her struggle to get her house back in order after a tornado, to clean out all the mud and broken glass that had blown in, to get the walls repapered, and so on: "I just worked like mad. I never stopped. And I know if it had been any other time I'd probably been in bed. But I just worked, just never did stop. There wasn't anything in this house that wasn't covered in mud and that didn't need scrubbing and drying and picking up. I just never slowed down."[204] It is of course painful to recognize that damage done may be irretrievable or even that it may take some time to get back to the status quo. The intolerance for the duration of the time when one will still be subject to the effects of an unwelcome event stimulates this speeding up and incessancy of activity. The speedy undoing of damage constitutes an approximation to denial after the event: we will get things back into such good order that it will be as if it had never happened.

There are also potentialities in human nature which everyday life does not summon into play, but which can be activated where something of crucial importance is at stake. Thus a father tells of his search for his little boy in the ruins of his house: "The first thing I thought of was coming here on account of this boy. And I commenced digging in the rubbish. I raised up the end of the wall. I'm injured by it yet. I raised something that two of us couldn't raise the next day.

I was excited, you know, and I guess I got supernatural strength. But I raised that section of wall and looked under that for him."[205]

In addition to the many factors already discussed which make for good will towards others following a disaster, there are wishes to be good, helpful, friendly, and loving, for which everyday life does not provide sufficient possibilities of satisfaction. One may contribute money to worthy causes, but this is impersonal and indirect; there is no contact with those whom one helps. On the other hand, those who ordinarily confront us as needing help often inspire suspicion rather than good will. Isn't the blind beggar a fraud who has a fortune stowed away? Is the man who falls down on the street ill or isn't he more likely drunk? But the need for help, and the justice of the claim for help, of those who have undergone a disaster are incontestable. And here is a chance to be of use in a more direct and personal way than is usually possible. As one active rescuer puts it: "I didn't have any superhuman strength or anything like that—just the desire to want to help. I would help anybody in anything like that, in a fire, in a storm, a flood, or any—or any way that I could lend help to anybody. I'm just turned that way—I would help them. It wouldn't necessarily have to be an emergency."[206] In this last reflection he seems to recognize that the impulse to help is there all the time, though it may require an extreme situation to give it adequate opportunity for expression.

I have spoken of those who are so hard hit that they manifest the "disaster syndrome" of depression and incapacitation, and of those less seriously affected who become absorbed in strenuous activity which serves to ward off painful feelings. It would seem also that some of those who live through an extreme danger situation without too severe damage experience a rapid alternation of positive and negative feelings, which are often not well observed or accurately remembered or reported. I should like to cite some instances of such fluctuations of emotion, which range from terror to elation, and which are apt to be oversimplified in retrospect. During and immediately following the event a survivor may be alternately alarmed by prospects of fatality and exhilarated by the sense of having escaped. Feelings of invulnerability and of helplessness recur in rapid succession. The interpretation of the event oscillates between catastrophe and miraculous escape. Later the image of what has happened and the attitude towards it become more stabilized, often with emphasis on the positive side. The leitmotiv which emerges in the post-disaster phase is: we were lucky. But let us examine now the earlier, more unstable emotional state.

The woman whom I have mentioned several times before, who tried so hard to remain calm throughout, retains nevertheless fairly detailed memories of a sequence of contrasting emotions. First alarmed by the tornado warnings, she speaks with a neighbor who tells her the best thing is to keep calm, and this makes her feel better. Then her married daughter picks up her baby, whom the mother had been taking care of, and drives away. She is left alone and is again uneasy. She then urges a neighbor to go to the school and bring her little girl home. With the child to take care of she again feels competent and in control. As the tornado descends she and the little girl take refuge in a closet. "I don't remember being scared at all. My little girl didn't get scared. 'Course we prayed. But we didn't have a scared feeling." The tornado brings the house down around them but leaves the closet standing. She cannot open the closet door because of the debris blown up against it and "I panicked for a second." However, the need to reassure the child helps her: "I kept saying, 'Now, Ellen May, don't be afraid. I'll get us out of here.' And I repeated that several times." Finally the closet door yields. But now there is a new danger of fallen electric wires about which she warns the child: " 'Don't step on any wires.' And I repeated that enough that she said, 'Mother, you sound like a broken record.' Well, I knew that she was still all right. She had not panicked." There follows a "funny" incident. She recalls that a day or two before her little girl had been asking for an old teddy bear, and she had not been able to remember where it was or whether she might not have given it away. Now suddenly amid the wreckage there was the lost teddy bear, blown down from the attic. Such incidents of unexpectedly finding belongings where so much has been destroyed and lost seem to produce moments of elation. It seems like a magical reassurance that one is lucky after all.

There follows a delayed feeling of alarm: "I'm sure that I must have been under shock. I felt a shock hit me after we got out of the closet and I didn't realize it, but I know now I must have been." As evidence of her shocked state she cites a futile effort to save something hopelessly damaged. She puts her camera, already soaked by the rain pouring into the roofless house, in a place where it will not get wet. She then goes out, and seeing the whole neighborhood laid waste, has the conviction she and her daughter are the sole survivors. There is the intense feeling of abandonment which we have already noted: "the loneliest feeling in the world." As she then sees some of her neighbors emerging from the ruins, and this terrible loneliness is suddenly overcome, she is "almost hysterical" but quickly reminds herself to remain calm. She proceeds to the nearby fire station where she borrows a fireman's hat and coat and goes out in the rain again to help others get to shelter or to the hospital. She retains in modified form the sense of being the sole survivor, in feeling that she alone is sufficiently intact to give the help that is needed. "Well, I thought that I was . . . it seemed that I was the only one that was—that I had a job that I had to do."

At the time that she arrived at the fire station, with the realization of having survived and not being alone, she experienced a phase of elation, which she later forgot but which was reported to her by one of the firemen. "I asked one of the firemen up there three or four days later, I said, 'Why in the world didn't you make me sit down and rest—out in the hail that afternoon?' He said, 'I asked you about fifteen minutes after you came here and put that hat and coat on. I asked you why you didn't get out of the hail, how you felt. And you told me you felt like a million dollars. And I thought anybody that felt like a million dollars after being in a tornado, well, I'd just leave them alone.' He said, 'I felt like you was doing all right.' " It would seem that this woman felt singled out by fate to be the sole survivor, but could not at first feel elated by this because it meant the sacrifice and loss of all the others. When to her great relief she found that others were still there, she could enjoy her feeling of being the chosen one without guilt. Understandably she cannot quite put into words her feeling about the uniqueness of her salvation which is combined with the fact of the others' also surviving: "It seemed that I was the only one that was ..." She cannot finish the sentence. We might guess that she felt she was the only one wholly saved, so that she alone had to take care of the others who were only partly saved. This combined feeling of being elect but not alone then became one of intense elation. Perhaps the contradictory ideas behind this feeling led to her forgetting it.

In this woman also the strenuous activity of helping others served to ward off awareness of damage to herself. She did not notice until afterwards that she was limping, that her leg was injured. The phase of elation and of stenuous activity subsequently give way to renewed anxiety. She begins to worry about her husband, son, and daughter, who were all out of town, and who might, out of anxiety to find out what had happened, drive back in too great haste and meet with an accident. Thus we see the instability of emotions in such a situation, where feelings of distress and the opposite succeed one another in rapid alternation.[207]

The doctor in Worcester, whose rescue efforts I have cited, gives a similar account of fluctuating emotional states. As the storm was blowing up he had gone out to his car to close the windows. It was then the tornado struck, and he ducked down on the floor of the car, pulling a sleeping bag over him. He congratulated himself that his little daughters had not come down to the car with him. As he felt the car being lifted and tossed, "I didn't think about being killed, but I didn't want to have my car turned over by a silly wind." Thus he tries to belittle the danger source and to displace concern for himself to his car. Recurrently, as we shall see, his feelings of well-being were closely bound up with the condition of the car. As the tornado passes, he thinks, "My goodness, I didn't blow away. I'm lucky." Getting out of the car, he sees his apartment house severely damaged, and he starts rushing up the stairs with "a real panicky feeling for my family." He shouts for his wife but she doesn't answer. "I felt badly then. Either she was gone or she was hurt so badly she couldn't answer. And my three kids..." These thoughts, as he ran through his devastated apartment, lasted "a very short space of time." Thus he does not deny that he imagined his family dead, but approximates denial by stressing the very brief duration of this thought. He decides they must have taken refuge in the basement and starts rushing downstairs again.

He then encounters a rather weak young man, a neighbor towards whom he has very friendly feelings, who is screaming that his baby is locked in his apartment, and is trying to break in the door, but "he's a very small, slight, skinny fellow" and he is ineffectual. The doctor stops to break in the door and reunite the young man with his baby. "That was really one of the few bits of uh—strong emotional feeling I saw. He grabbed the kid and let out this howl of relief, 'My baby! my baby!'" We may guess that this act of rescue, of restoring a child to its father, for which he interrupted his search for his own family, may have served as a propitiatory act and a magical insurance that he would find his wife and children safe. And he does find them in the basement, barefoot and covered with dirt, but unharmed. The children when they see him begin to whimper. "And I picked them up and felt very sorry for them and very guilty that I hadn't been closer by." They had actually been in the apartment when the windows shattered and all sorts of debris had blown in, and had only run down to the basement afterwards. He finds the thought of their exposure to such danger, without his being there to take care of them, very painful for some time afterwards. "As I thought of them standing in the kitchen... with glass flying around in the air, brickbats and pieces of cars, which we found later, I just couldn't bear the thought." However, as they return to their apartment, and he and his wife compare their experiences, the sense of having come through unscathed assumes the ascendancy, "and I felt sort of exhilarated." As they notice the ruined meat loaf in the oven, "I was joking with my wife, something about a hell of a time to have a tornado just when we were having meat for a change."

He then goes out to see what he can do for others, "and I was glad I was a doctor, I could help these wounded people I knew there would be." There is a confident feeling of his own intactness and power to help where others are damaged and helpless. This feeling, however, gives way to a sense of his own vulnerability as he enters the destroyed area and becomes aware of wires down, gas escaping, the danger of fire, "and that made me feel scared . . . I felt tense at that time . . . I noticed that I was trembling, and I felt excited. But I also felt very clearheaded and thought I knew what to do." Thus he quickly reenforces his sense of competence and control, to ward off feelings of alarm and the awareness of his vulnerability. In his tour of the destroyed area, which I have already described, he had a sense of others, whether injured or not, being disoriented and incapacitated for useful activity. But his contrasting confidence in his own lucidity and competence gave way after some time as he began to realize that his efforts to help were proving largely ineffective. "And I felt frustrated and angry that I thought I could do something and it turned out I could do practically nothing." He feels "extremely tired and increasingly useless."

As he returns to his family, the saved sector of the world again becomes central and there is another phase of euphoria. His car had been blown into a position where its front wheels were resting on the back of another car. He hails a group of passing boys and they are delighted to help him extricate the car. When he finds then that the motor still runs, "I felt exhilarated and I was stimulated." Here was something that could be successfully restored, his car whose intactness renewed his sense of invulnerability. And instead of overextending himself in efforts to assist others, he could himself get help for a change. Also people from outside were coming in to look at all the damage, and "they were horror-stricken.

I didn't feel horror-stricken any longer." He has again an advantage over others who are undergoing painful feelings from which he has recovered. "To give you an idea how euphoric I felt: people were passing by, and I mockingly scolded the girls (his little daughters) for playing around so vigorously and causing all this mess." That is, he jokingly pretends that all the wreckage has been caused by the children playing too wildly. Some of those who had been through the ordeal laughed at this joke, but the outsiders failed to find it funny. He then sets out in the car with his family and some neighbors and takes great pleasure in the amazement of the passersby at seeing the car with its battered chassis running nevertheless. "I found it amusing and so did my wife and some other people that came with us to ride out, and we would make jokes back and forth like 'there's nothing like a Ford' and so on."

With nightfall, after they have found a temporary refuge, distressing feelings reemerge. "I couldn't sleep. I kept seeing all those wounded people and I felt terrible." Apprehensive and depressed feelings persist and become intensified in the following days. He feels that at a sharp word or a noise he might "burst into tears or become angry." He is haunted by the "image of all the shambles and the thoughts of my little girls and my wife and my little son in that murderous room." The picture of what might have happened assumes the ascendancy over the realization of having survived unscathed. The sense of impotence to help, which overcame him as he first went through the devastated area, manifests itself also at the hospital afterwards. "Everybody in the hospital seemed depressed and under-productive, lacking in energy." Further restitution is required to reinstate more positive feelings. "It wasn't until I replaced my car with a brand new shiny car that I felt all together again."[208]

Thus such an extreme experience may provoke a transient emotional imbalance, with rapid mood swings between elation and despair. We have here in normal individuals a condition which approximates a temporary manic-depressive psychosis, precipitated by the pressure of circumstances. One might suppose that being tossed back and forth between hopeful and pessimistic feelings would be appropriate to the situation where danger is still impending or has not yet passed over, when the individual cannot know what will be his fate or that of his loved ones. However, as we have seen, in the phases of anticipation and impact there is apt to be considerable denial and inhibition of emotion. The more violent ups and downs of feeling seem to set in afterwards, when the danger is past and the result is known. One has survived, one's family is uninjured, and then one has delayed scare reactions, alternating with feelings of triumph and invulnerability. It is as if we find at a later moment the fluctuations of hope and fear which would have been appropriate to the danger situation when the outcome was still uncertain. But at that time it would have been too painful to submit to the full force of these contrasting emotions. Thus they are postponed to the time after the event. The warded-off apprehension of what might happen emerges in shuddering thoughts of what could have happened. The image of fatalities that did not occur alternates with the sense of miraculous escape. As we shall see, these alternations of euphoric and discouraged feelings may continue, though at a slower tempo, for some time afterwards.

There are various circumstances in disasters and different individual predispositions which may make for particularly elated feelings. I have already spoken of the festive atmosphere that may prevail in a situation of threatening danger (as that of a rising flood) while there is still no belief that any serious damage will materialize. We have also observed the occasional occurrence of orgiastic release following disaster, or in a persisting situation of danger, from the feeling, for instance, that one has become exempted from moral rules, or as a defense by indulgence against a sense of deprivation. In the cases just cited, of the women from San Angelo and the doctor from Worcester, the fact of having undergone extreme danger and emerging unscathed occasioned moments of triumph and intensely euphoric feelings. Such reenforcement of one's sense of invulnerability is particu-

larly apt to occur among persons who have lived through a
danger situation without any damage or loss. So, for instance,
vacationers who are caught in a hurricane and come out
afterwards to find the only damage is that to property, which
is not their own, tend to feel highly euphoric.

Some other instances of elation in disaster may be cited.
In the destruction of Hiroshima, a professor from the university and his son were pinned down under the ruins of
their house and, as the house caught fire, were in imminent
danger of burning to death. As a Japanese informant relates
the incident, as told to him later, "His (the professor's) son
said, 'Father, we can do nothing except make our mind up
to consecrate our lives for the country. Let us give *Banzai* to
our Emperor!' Then the father followed after his son, '*Tenno-
heika, Banzai, Banzai, Banzai!*' In the result Dr. Hiraiwa
said, 'Strange to say, I felt calm and bright and peaceful
spirit in my heart, when I chanted *Banzai* to Tenno.' After-
ward his son got out and digged down and pulled out his
father and thus they were saved. In thinking of their experience of that time Dr. Hiraiwa repeated, 'What a fortunate
(thing) that we are Japanese! It was my first time I ever
tasted such a beautiful spirit when I decided to die for our
Emperor.' "[209] We may suppose that in this account by a
Japanese of exaltation in extremity there may be the same
improvement on reality as we suspected in some of the accounts of Americans about their indestructible calm. It is
ideal behavior which is being described, which may have
been more or less approximated in the event. However, where
such feelings do occur as those described above, there seems
to be an anticipation of union in death with a beloved parent
figure. This expectation negates the sense of abandonment;
there is the feeling that the greatest and most beloved power
is with us and we with him. The terror of dying helpless and
forsaken is transformed into the opposite: elation triumphs
over despair.

Under certain circumstances for some individuals the experience of an extreme event may have an unconscious significance which is highly gratifying. William James speaks of

the intense pleasure he experienced in the San Francisco earthquake. He was staying at Stanford at the time, so that he was outside the most severely damaged area. Neither he nor any member of his family was injured, and he could also feel free from disturbing involvement in that he was an outsider, a visitor in the community. In these circumstances there was little to interfere with the delight which being shaken by the earthquake aroused in him. As he relates, when "I felt my bed begin to waggle, my first consciousness was one of gleeful recognition of the nature of the movement." The shaking becomes more violent; he tries to get up and is thrown down again; furniture crashes and the plaster of the walls cracks. All this inspires a feeling of "glee at the vividness which such an abstract verbal term as 'earthquake' could put on when translated into sensible reality and verified concretely . . . I felt no trace of fear; it was pure delight and welcome. 'Go it,' I almost cried aloud, 'and go it stronger!' "

Thus "earthquake" which had been up until then only a word for him becomes a real thing. For someone like William James, professionally occupied with words, this was an escape from his usual level of experience where words generally (not only the word "earthquake") may often have seemed empty. A breakthrough of something real, an overpowering wordless force that takes hold of one, was for him a favorable departure from the level of everyday life. His reaction is the opposite of that often encountered where, for people who find their everyday life sufficiently real, such an abrupt break is apt to seem unreal.

William James goes on to give his personal associations to the earthquake, which provide a clue to the special pleasure he derived from it. Before he had left Boston for his California visit, a friend of his, B., had said, "I hope they'll give you a touch of earthquake while you're there, so that you may also become acquainted with that California custom." Thus, "I personified the earthquake . . . It was the earthquake of my friend B's augury, which had been lying low and holding itself back during the intervening months, in order, on that lustrous April morning, to invade my room, and energize the more intensely and triumphantly. It came, moreover, directly to me. It stole in behind my back, and once inside the room, had me all to itself, and could manifest itself convincingly."[210] In this account we may discern a very slightly disguised, though unconscious, homosexual fantasy: the earthquake which comes to him in such a personal way, stealing up from behind and having him all to itself, is felt to be a representative of his friend (it was "B's earthquake" as he puts it at another point). The potentiality for this intense experience has been "lying low and holding itself back." That is, as we may interpret it, his homosexual impulses have been inhibited. And it is perhaps as a result of such repression that everyday life has seemed emotionally impoverished, a thing of mere words. The assault of the earthquake, since it came irresistibly and without his having to feel responsible, could gratify, under a disguise, otherwise impermissible longings.

What we might call a secondary gain of disaster, which may bring with it feelings of euphoria, is a temporary exemption from usual tasks and responsibilities. Hans Castorp, in *The Magic Mountain*, felt peculiarly elated when he learned he had a slight touch of tuberculosis and would have to remain at the sanitorium, where he had come as a visitor and whose mode of life had already charmed him. The worrisome responsibility of pursuing his career was temporarily lifted. He felt as he had in school as a boy when he had been told that he would not be promoted; no further effort had to be made for the rest of the term. An episode expressing this sense of emancipation is related from the recent flood in Holland. Two school teachers, stranded on the upper stories of their houses, called back and forth to each other from their windows. They had both been recently concerned about making applications for a more advanced position. They now asked each other laughingly: "Are you still going to apply?" As they looked down at the flood waters which had effectively disrupted usual routines, they evidently felt a welcome sense of the unimportance, at least for the time being, of academic aspirations.[211]

In a disaster, as in less dramatic misfortunes, humor may be used as a defense against distress. We have noted the joking remark of the doctor from Worcester about the ruined meat loaf: What a time to have a tornado, just when for once we were going to have meat for supper! Thus he pretends to overlook the destruction of the whole apartment, not to mention the more widespread devastation, as if the whole catastrophe consisted in the loss of the meat loaf. In a similar way he reduces a great to a small thing when he jokingly pretends that all the wreckage has been caused by his little girls playing too wildly. In playfully rebuking the children for making such a mess, he equates the destruction wrought by a terrible force of nature with the breakage of household objects by children who play too carelessly. Thus a humorous attitude for the moment reduces great misfortunes to something small and harmless.[212] Another, related joking device consists in the pretense of mistaking the deprivational for the gratifying. In this spirit a woman with a bandaged head jokes about having got a fine new Easter bonnet. When her husband and son, who were separated from her during the tornado, finally find her in the hospital, "I never will forget how they looked. I tell you of course I looked awful. I tried to pass it off, you know. They had a little old thing wrapped around my head. I told my husband, 'I didn't get an Easter bonnet, but I got one after all.' I tried to be funny, you know, where it wouldn't tear them up so bad."[213]

Part III:
Aftermath

1.
The tormenting memory

AN EXPERIENCE of extreme danger is not over once the danger is past, even for those who survive it intact. Something has intruded into their emotional life which it requires some time to assimilate. And this is the more so, of course, to the degree to which the individual has suffered damage or loss. Following a catastrophic event people are apt to find themselves forced to relive it over and over again in memory. This reliving, though painful, seems to have in many cases a curative effect as the feelings of extreme distress associated with the event are gradually extinguished through repeated exposure in imagination.

As contrasted with this process of recovery through repetition, we may note two opposite variants. For some the experience has been so unbearable that there is an effort to repress it completely. In the extreme instance this leads to amnesia. In other instances, the effort towards repression does not succeed in obliterating the memory, but the individual may struggle to avoid all reminders of the experience, whose reevocation he finds intolerable. He cannot speak of it, he does not want to hear about it, he avoids the scene of the disaster. At the opposite extreme from that of repression, we find the individual who continues to be haunted by the painful experience without any reduction of distressing feelings. He cannot, as we say, get over it, and it continues to absorb most of his thoughts and energies.

As disaster victims describe the way in which the memory of the event persistently recurs: "It's a thing you try to dispel from your mind, but you just won't let it. The thought is continual."[214] "Oh Lord! that (the tornado) is all I do think about, unless I'm talking to somebody about something else. I can just see that wall coming apart and them windows coming in every time I shut my eyes."[215] "I just simply got hysterical, you know, 'cause I get to thinking about it, thinking how awful it was, and what I had to go through there in those few minutes."[216] "It doesn't bother me to talk about it, as long as I don't lie down at night and think about it. Then I relive it all again."[217]

It is a common clinical observation that the revival of painful experiences may have a curative effect, yet the process involved remains somewhat obscure. Freud, in *Beyond the Pleasure Principle*, reflected on the tendency to repeat painful experiences. One of the motives he observed was that of mastering the initial experience, which had been undergone involuntarily and passively, by assuming an active role in the repetition. Thus a small child, who has suffered from his mother's leaving him, repeatedly throws a favored toy away from him: in the separation which he reenacts in play, he substitutes an active role for his original passive one. At the same time he inures himself, by the repeated exposure, to the painful event. In the more complicated play of dramatic tragedy, we may see a similar mechanism at work. The playwright sets in action, and the audience voluntarily expose themselves to, terrible happenings in which they reexperience in a disguised form the misfortunes of their own lives.

The haunting memories of a catastrophe rise in the mind unbidden, so that, in contrast to play (childish or theatrical), they do not offer the advantage of transforming passivity into activity. However, they provide the possibility of gradually inuring oneself to an initially overwhelming experience. With repeated exposure in imagination, one may react with reduced distress. Also many of the feelings which the event stimulates only emerge afterwards, especially if the catastrophe has occurred suddenly, and because one tries to deny and ward off painful feelings in the moment of impact. There seems to be no advantageous way of abridging the emotional distress related to an extreme event. A certain amount of painful feeling must be undergone before a stable recovery is achieved. The same applies to the process of mourning for beloved persons. Attempts to avoid, by repression or affectlessness, the due course of grief, and the sad work of undoing the relationship which must be given up, only lead to delayed reactions and more morbid equivalents of the warded off distress.

The need for subsequent reexposure in memory to a disastrous event is proportional to the lack of antecedent preparation. Anticipation involves exposing oneself in imagination beforehand so that the event does not take one wholly by surprise and the edge is taken off its most terrifying effects. To the extent that there has not been this inurement in advance, the work of achieving tolerance for the experience afterwards is greater. We see here how persistence in denial or in withholding emotional response in relation to an oncoming danger makes for greater difficulty in recovering after it has materialized.

The inability to react adequately to a sudden extreme event at the moment when it strikes (the influx of strong stimuli being more than one can assimilate) makes for delayed reactions. The tendency towards denial, which may persist for some time afterwards, as in feelings that it is all unreal, contributes to the same effect. Disaster victims, as well as those who come in from nearby and are confronted with unaccustomed sights of devastation, are frequently quite conscious of this inability to react immediately. As a young man coming into a tornado-stricken city says: "It couldn't dawn on me all at once."[218] Those who are occupied in intensive activity immediately following the disaster ward off during that time distressing feelings which will, however, emerge later. A fireman relates: "There was dead bodies lying all

around, but we just snaked the hose around 'em. It's funny—
I didn't think nothing about it then. But later on when I
thought about it, it made me weak-kneed."[219]

There is the German legend of the man who drove his
carriage at night across the frozen Lake Constance, mistaking
it for solid ground. Arriving at the inn on the far side, he
was greeted with amazement, as all the roads were blocked
with snow. Asked how he had come, he pointed back to the
course he had taken. When he was told it was the lake over
which he had driven, he was so struck with fright that he
fell dead on the spot. This story contains a psychological truth exemplified not only in the case of dangers of which
one was unaware at the time, but also in those where full
emotional response was inhibited at the moment of greatest
threat. One may then experience an intense scare reaction in
retrospect, after the danger is past. Disaster victims tend to
be occupied with thoughts of what could have happened,
which they have by one or another fortunate chance escaped.
The following instance approximates that of the rider over
Lake Constance, since those involved were unaware of the
hazard that might have destroyed them until it was past. A
young couple had just left the trailer in which they lived
when it was struck by a tornado, whirled high into the air
and shattered to bits. They did not see this and did not know
of the tornado's passage until they returned some time later
to find their trailer vanished and to hear from others how
it had been destroyed. The young man expresses the subsequent feelings of shock from imagining what would have
happened had they been at home at the crucial moment: "I
think the idea of what could have possibly happened sort of
jarred us more than the loss of the material things. It seemed
after looking around there and seeing what it did to the general neighborhood, a person just sort of, kind of—well, now
if I'd been in that trailer, if I'd blown to pieces or something . . ."[220]

For others, who recognize that they are in a danger situation at the time, there are still likely to be scare reactions
afterwards, which may be more intense than those experi-

enced in the moment of actual peril. This, as I have said, is related to the suddenness of the event (one cannot "take it in" so quickly) and to defenses against acknowledging unwelcome events and painful feelings. As the disaster agitates its victims after it has passed, the strain of its recurrent presence in imagination may evoke renewed defenses. A woman, for instance, tells how she had a fainting fit three days after the tornado which severely damaged the house she was in. "I was sick at my stomach all night. The next morning was when I fainted. I just blacked out. . . But this was the third day after the tornado. I hadn't slept any the first night, not too much the second night. In fact, until I fainted, you know, or blacked out, well, I don't think I really slept."[221] Thus, to exclude the continued stimulation of the not yet assimilated event which was allowing her no rest, she was forced as she puts it to "black out."

People not only think repeatedly about a disastrous experience afterwards, they are also apt to talk a great deal about it: "We can't talk about anything else. We just reminisce this storm. And I don't know how long it will go on, but you don't know anything else, it seems, to talk about."[222] Speaking about the disaster, in contrast to being haunted by memories that come against one's will, provides the possibility of turning passivity into activity. In retelling an experience, we voluntarily reevoke it. Narration is thus like play in that one can assume control over the repetition of an event which in its occurrence ran counter to one's wishes. While, alone at night, one may dread the vivid revival of the experience, when telling it to others one wants to evoke it as vividly as possible. Here is again the turning of passivity into activity: from being the helpless victim one becomes the effective story teller, and it is the others, the audience, who are made to undergo the experience. The greater orderliness of a verbal account as compared with inchoate and bewildering impressions is also reassuring. And one may revise the event in various ways which make it more tolerable, omitting certain details, embellishing others, transforming parts of the experience in a humorous way and so on.

Public legend thus begins to replace private suffering. The response of others provides a rectification of the initial experience, undergone alone. The feeling of abandonment in the moment of impact is assuaged by reliving the experience with sympathetic listeners. In a common disaster, the feeling afterwards that one is not alone is enhanced by the fact that others have been through the same thing. When one has suffered a misfortune singly, one's response to sympathizers may be complicated by a sense of envy and resentment that they are untouched. Among survivors of a disaster, recounting their similar experiences, there is a more unmixed fellow-feeling.

Thoughts and talk about a disaster afterwards are occupied to a large extent with what one might have done or should have done but did not do. The fact of having come through unscathed does not preclude intensive occupation with hazards barely escaped and what one should have done to protect oneself better. One woman who was in her car when the tornado hit and who was unharmed reflects: "You know when you get to thinking about anything, you can think, well, this could have happened, and how narrow maybe you did escape. I get to thinking sometimes, I sat up there under the steering wheel. I didn't lay down in the seat and try to protect myself from a board that could have come through the windshield, which didn't come through."[223] Another woman tells how in the night following the tornado she discussed with her neighbor what he should have done. He and his family had taken refuge in a corner of the house, which happened to suffer the severest damage. Even though none of them was injured, the neighbor woman scolds him: " 'Jimmy, you shouldn't have done that—the thing to have done was to stand right in the middle of the floor.' . . . So we talked about it all the rest of the night, you know. How we should have done and what we didn't do."[224] This woman had herself tried to persuade her son that they should run to their neighbors' house as the storm grew in violence, and they had still been arguing about it when their own house blew down. In telling her neighbor what he should have done differently she was apparently working off her own regrets for not having acted sooner (since as it turned out the neighbors' house was much less damaged than her own).

A sudden disaster both mobilizes a powerful urge towards activity and allows it very little scope. The disaster victim has been able to do so little just at the moment when he felt maximal activity was called for. It is these frustrated impulses towards activity which express themselves in the recurrent fantasies of what one should have done that one omitted to do. Thus actions uncompleted, as well as emotional responses which were inhibited, at the time form part of the reliving of the event in retrospect.[225] There is also a sense of protest at one's having been so helpless in the danger situation. It would be more in keeping with the ideal of oneself as being in control of one's fate (particularly important perhaps for Americans) if one were to escape through one's own competence rather than by luck. Thus it is not enough that a board did not crash through the windshield; one should have put oneself in such a position as to be untouched if it did. There may also be a deeper-lying motive for this preoccupation with what one should have done but omitted to do. Recalling again the tendency to take disaster as a punishment, I would suggest that the conscience of the disaster victim may be exercised about other things which he failed to do, the performance of which might have saved him from undergoing this chastisement. These unconscious regrets for moral insufficiency may assume the conscious guise of repetitive preoccupation with what one should have done but omitted to do in the disaster situation itself.

While there is an impulse to revive a disturbing experience in order to get a belated mastery of it, the painfulness of this revival also stimulates the wish to avoid it.[226] Often the compensations of reliving the experience in talking about it to others counteract the inclination towards suppression or repression. However, there are some individuals for whom this is not the case, who cannot speak (for a briefer or longer time), and cannot bear to hear about the catastrophe. A mother tells about her little girl who was at school when the tornado hit, that afterwards "she wouldn't talk to us. It was the third day before we really knew everything that happened. When they brought her in after my nephew found her, she wouldn't say a word. And she wouldn't talk about it that night, and the next day she just turned and walked off when it was mentioned. . . She just stood around and seemed like there was something on her mind. She didn't play like she usually does, or talk. She's quite a talker, her normal self." The mother adds that for her own part, "the first two or three days I wasn't capable of talking to her at all. I was too upset myself."[227] Another woman relates, "I couldn't even talk about it last year. If I'd go down town people would go to question me—I'd jerk at them half the time. Couldn't talk about it last year. People in stores would go to asking me questions and I got so I didn't even want to go to town."[228] Expressing her intolerance for hearing about the disaster afterwards, another woman says, "I even got up and went from one room to the other to keep from hearing them talk about it. Last night they got to talking about Johnny (her grandson who was killed) and about the storm after supper there, and I told my youngest daughter, I said, I just had the creeps. My hands got so cold, just got so nervous. I just wanted them to hush. I just felt like screaming. 'Don't ever mention that storm again!'—that's the way I felt."[229]

In such reactions there seems to be the feeling that if one will just be quiet, the terrible memories will go away. Others' talking about the event, or asking one to talk about it, is experienced as a threat, a conjuring up of what has happened and subjecting one to it all over again. We see here two opposite ways of feeling about words. Words may relieve distress, becoming a less disturbing substitute for the event described. Or words may act to conjure up the event in all its force, in which case they should not be spoken. The person who does not want to speak about what has happened, or hear it spoken of, is hoping to repress it rather than to inure himself to it by reexposure. That this effort at repression is often unsuccessful is attested to, for instance, by the woman who could not bear to hear her children talking about the tornado. She is the same one who acknowledged: "Oh Lord! that's all I do think about," and told how every time she closed her eyes she saw the walls falling in on her.

There is another hazard in hearing other people talk about a catastrophe which one has suffered: they may talk about it in the wrong way. In mastering a painful experience, each individual may have his own preferred method. In the effort to avoid pain, one tries to dose one's reexposure to the event according to one's own idiosyncratic tolerance. Certain details may be more unbearable than others and one tries to put off facing them. One gets used to what has happened a little at a time, thinking one day of an injury narrowly escaped, and the next of a prized possession that was lost. But when other people talk about it, they may bring up just the things of which one was happily forgetful at the moment or not yet ready to think about. There are different ways of reconciling oneself to misfortune, and what is consoling for one may not be so for another. Such discrepancies appear, for instance, in a family where the children do not like to hear the grown-ups discussing the disaster, though they will talk about it themselves. According to one mother's observation, "If someone comes in from out of town and we talk about it, well, they (the children) will say, 'Let's don't talk about it.' Because it reminds them, I guess. But still they'll talk about it among themselves and not seem to think too much about it. But if they hear older people discussing it, they'd rather you didn't talk about it."[230]

The particular circumstances of a disaster may make it difficult for members of a family to talk about it together. In the town of Vicksburg, Mississippi, a tornado struck on a Saturday afternoon and severely damaged a movie theatre filled with children, many of them there without their parents. Some children were killed; others were buried in the debris for hours before they were rescued. Afterwards many parents in the town expressed a strong feeling against talking with their children about what had happened. They thought the terrible event would be most quickly forgotten if nothing was said about it.[231] Parents whose children underwent this ordeal apart from them probably felt guilty for not having been there. That such an event should have struck with special force at the children may have made the parents of the town generally (even those whose children were not in the theatre that afternoon) feel shaken in their capacity for providing protection. Such feelings of guilt towards children and weakened confidence in one's ability to protect them are understandably difficult for parents to acknowledge to their children. Also the fact of death had intruded itself abruptly into the children's sphere. Most of the children of the town knew some child who was killed. But death is a subject which parents generally have difficulty in discussing with their children, and about which they are apt not to be very candid. So, for instance, if a child asks whether he could die, parents frequently say that children do not die, that one only dies when one gets very old. Such reassurances are disproved when one is forcibly confronted with the death of children. In such a situation parents are apt to feel painfully helpless, deprived of their usually trusted means of protecting children against fear. It is also often the case that in relation to children adults believe in the dangerous, conjuring power of words rather than in their more benevolent effects. There are other subjects besides danger and death, notably sex, about which it is often felt that if one does not say anything then the children will not think about it. This is a general factor which, together with the special ones suggested, may have contributed to the preference of these parents for silence about the disastrous event.

Other special circumstances may facilitate talking about the disaster afterwards. Among these, in contrast to the Vicksburg experience, there would be the situation of parents being together with their children and protecting them effectively. We may recall the woman from San Angelo, for instance, who had her little daughter brought home from school when she heard the tornado warning, who took refuge with the child in a closet where they both escaped injury though the house fell down around them, and where on coming out they found amid the wreckage the little girl's missing teddy bear that had blown down from the attic. We can readily imagine that it would be easy for this mother and child to talk together about their experience afterwards. The mother could feel satisfied with the way in which she fulfilled her maternal role, she and her little girl came through in good shape (the mother stressed that neither of them became fearful or excited), and there were some bits of special luck, so prized at such times.

Those who strive to avoid the revival of a painful event may resort to a variety of defenses. I have mentioned the attempt to ward off stimuli which might recall what has happened: not to hear it spoken of, not to see the signs of destruction. Such avoidance may be temporary and may be followed by a gradually increasing tolerance for the memory of the disaster. There may also be a more or less protracted apathy, or a paradoxical sense of well-being, where the individual is unable to feel the distress appropriate to what he has undergone.

Where a beloved person has died, a peculiarly painful siege of memory besets the survivor. The acceptance of the loss involves what Freud has called the work of mourning: reviving one by one the memories associated with the dead, saying as it were goodbye to each, and so gradually detaching one's feelings from him.[232] Attempts to elude or abridge this painful process are not successful. The grief that has been warded off is likely to break through on some later occasion.[233] The effort to escape from the immediate distress may be penalized by more severe disturbances. Thus Lindemann cites the case of a young man who, following the death of his wife in the Cocoanut Grove fire, was at first cheerful and hyperactive. This mood was soon followed by one of extreme agitation (the young man in fact blamed himself for not having been able to save his wife) which ended in suicide.[234]

The most thoroughgoing defense against the revival of a disturbing experience is that of blotting it out from memory completely, in developing amnesia for what has happened. As we know from the work on war neuroses, this pathological defense (which is also attended by other symptoms) is one which requires undoing. The repressed memories must be brought back to consciousness so that the individual can recover from the trauma by the painful process of reliving it which he had tried too abruptly to escape.[235]

Efforts at denial after a disastrous event are indicative of an antecedent emotional state where energies are already absorbed to a great extent in internal conflicts and are thus not free or not adequate for the work of mastering the new difficulty. The warding off of feeling or recollection then leads to further disturbances. The painful experience can only be mastered by repeated confrontation in memory and gradual inurement and acceptance.

I should now like to sum up the significance of denial in various phases of a disaster. In relation to a possible future disaster at some remote date, those who are free from severe neurotic anxiety tend to deny the danger: it will not happen, or it will not affect them, or they just do not react to the prospect with any feeling of worry. The tendency to continue these attitudes at a time when a disaster is imminent has negative consequences in that the traumatic effect of the event when it does occur is bound to be greater to the extent that there has not been emotional preparation for it. In the moment of impact denial again assumes a benevolent aspect in that those who retain the illusion of their own invulnerability while undergoing extreme danger tend to come out of it with less subsequent disturbance than those in whom this illusion is shattered. After the event denial again assumes a negative sign. Avoidance of response to what has happened or of the memory of it is indicative of a disturbed emotional state and induces further disturbance.

We might construct hypothetically on this basis two alternative sequences of attitudes, the most adaptive and the least adaptive. The individual who will, as far as the variable being considered is concerned, weather a disaster most advantageously is, to begin with, sufficiently free of neurotic anxiety that he does not worry about remote dangers. However, he is able to shift when a danger is imminent so that he takes it seriously, even while others are saying, and perhaps quite justly, that it may still not happen. He pictures the event to himself, and besides planning any relevant precautions, begins to inure himself to its emotional impact in this imaginary pre-exposure. He experiences some of the feelings appropriate to it in advance, which protects him against being overwhelmed by the unforeseen. Partly as a result of this preparation, partly because of more long-term favorable factors (e.g. not needing to feel omnipotent in order not to feel destroyed), in the moment of extreme danger he preserves his confidence in his own survival. Afterwards he is able to acknowledge the full extent of the hazards undergone and whatever losses he may have suffered. He can tolerate the revival of the experience in memory, together with the painful feelings thus aroused; he can talk about it, and, by reexposure in imagination, will gradually assimilate the event so that it can be looked back upon with equanimity.

In the opposite picture, there is the individual who worries about remote catastrophes, representing to himself under this guise components of his own personality which rouse anxiety, such as explosive hostility precariously held in check or punitive self-condemnation. When danger becomes imminent, however, it threatens to rouse unbearable alarm since real hazards assume the monstrous forms of his troubled fantasy. The catastrophes which he could face as long as they seemed relatively remote can no longer be contemplated when they seem close at hand. Thus he wards off too great alarm by denying the imminent danger. In the moment of impact he is overwhelmed partly because of lack of preparation just beforehand, partly because of negative pre-disposing factors of a more long term sort. For instance, if he suffers from intense guilt feelings and apprehension of punishment, when danger overtakes him he may be convinced that he is about to pay the extreme penalty for his sins. He is overcome with terror, face to face with death. Afterwards he cannot bear the revival of this devastating experience; he will not speak of it, or may become apathetic with feelings of unreality about what has happened; or he may repress it altogether. The continuing tension produced by the unassimilated trauma will then occasion further difficulties.

These are two hypothetical cases. There are fourteen other possible combinations of denial and non-denial in the four phases of a disaster. I leave it for the reader to fill in these alternative possibilities, and, more important, to look for their exemplification in life.

In the period following a disaster, the task of assimilating the excessive stimulation recently experienced occasions a number of disturbances. The individual is tense and restless, unable to suspend the effects of his experience. In consequence there are apt to be sleeping difficulties; one cannot relax. When one does sleep, often there is no escape from the revival of the traumatic event, which is vividly repeated in nightmares. Absorption of energies in the working over of the painful experience makes for inattentiveness to what is currently going on and for incapacitation for other activities. As one disaster victim puts it, "I haven't been able to sleep or work or think since it happened. I just keep going over and over it in my mind."[236] The event to which one could not fully react at the time continues afterwards to demand its emotional due and evokes feelings of apprehensiveness. These are often associated, as we shall see, with anticipations of another disaster. The urge to action so incompletely carried out in the suddenness of the event contributes to restlessness and irritability.

Ordinarily people recover spontaneously from these distresses. The intensity of reaction to the remembered event gradually wanes. However, in some cases this does not happen. A woman describes how a year after a disaster she remains preoccupied with it. Her home which was destroyed by the tornado has been rebuilt and she did not lose any members of her family. However, she seems unable to forget; her energies remain absorbed in going over what happened to the extent that her relations to people have become impoverished. She is withdrawn and apparently depressed. She says that, before the tornado, "I had company and I'd always enjoy it. And now when somebody comes, I just can't hardly wait for them to go. At times I act like I used to before the storm, and then again seems like that's just all I do, you know, just sit around and think about what I went through and everything."[237]

Such inability to recover from a traumatic experience is related to pre-existing emotional disturbances. To mention one or two possibilities, an individual may be particularly dependent on protective powers; he may strive to be good and to hold down any rebellious tendencies in the hope that, in return, he will always be taken care of. The occurrence of a disaster shatters these expectations. The powers are not protective, they do not love him. And this may be because he is unworthy of love; they have discerned his underlying bad impulses which he had so sacrificially restrained. Disillusionment with the protective powers, feeling oneself unloved and unlovable is expressed in depression. Masochistic tendencies may also contribute to prolonged preoccupation with a disastrous experience since it is unconsciously gratifying. Any antecedent neurotic disturbance makes for difficulty in the mastery of a trauma. The individual's energies are largely preempted by repressed impulses and defenses against them. Thus he does not have energy free for the new emotional task of assimilating the painful experience. The intrusion of a traumatic event into the neurotic situation, by making a new demand on emotional energies, may unbalance the defensive structure. Inhibited impulses may threaten to break through, rousing anxiety, and calling for further defensive measures. The result may be the precipitation of a more severe neurosis.[238]

2.
The fear of recurrence

ONE OF THE most common reactions of people who have undergone a disaster is the fear that it will happen again.[239] A doctor in Worcester tells how, shortly after the tornado, he approached an injured woman who was wandering about amid the ruins and offered to help her: "The only thing she said was, 'Will it come back? I'm afraid it's going to come back!' "[240] Here there seems to be uncertainty about the duration of activity of a destructive force. When a disastrous event has just occurred an atmosphere of danger prevails. This sense of continued threat from the original destructive agency may persist for longer or shorter periods, depending on the nature of the catastrophe and the susceptibilities of the individual. Just after a tornado, for instance, people may feel apprehensively that it has not yet spent its force and will imminently strike again.

However, when the disastrous event is recognized as having reached its end, there is also apt to be a strong expectation that it will be followed by another just like it. Thus throughout the year following the tornado in San Angelo the people of the stricken town were recurrently fearful that there would be another. As one woman puts it, "I think everybody out here, or who have been through one anywhere

(151)

I guess, have such a horror of having to go through the same thing again. Now, I know that all my neighbors around here and everybody I have talked to that live out here, they say that when it comes up a cloud they just can't hardly stand it, if it looks like there's any wind in it. They have to keep watching to see if it's going to look like the other cloud, the tornado cloud. They're worried because maybe there will be another one. After you have been through one, I think anyone feels that way. It's just something you never forget."[241] And another woman from San Angelo says, "There's a fear you can't conquer after seeing that, at least I can't... When I see a storm coming up now, you always imagine there is destruction in it, even if it is a rain storm."[242]

A newcomer in a town which previously underwent a severe tornado remarks on this continual apprehension of recurrence, which he, who was not there at the time of the disaster, does not share: "These people are tornado-happy. Every time a dark cloud comes up they go into their caves. A fellow can walk into a beer tavern on Saturday night and say, 'There's a storm coming up,' and empty the place in a minute."[243] In Texas City following the explosion, "the same people who had been so callous to the actual threat of the burning Grandcamp (the ship which blew up) were now sensitized to any suggestions of threat. The alarm, 'Get out of town—there's going to be another explosion,' was repeated again and again."[244] Among the rumors which circulate following a disaster, one of the most frequent is that some further catastrophe is imminent.[245] After the supposedly impregnable dikes in Kansas City had been overwhelmed by a flood, the rumor went around that an old Indian had predicted not only this flood but a greater one which would soon follow.[246]

Commenting on this fear of recurrence and its lack of relation to objective probability, Franz Alexander cited his own experience in having his apartment broken into by burglars, who threatened him at gun point and tied him up while they ransacked the place. Although at the time he was calm and observant, the following evening he was filled with appre-

hension of another robbery. Despite reflections that this was
highly unlikely, he felt impelled to take every precaution he
could think of to guard against burglars breaking in again.[247]

It would seem that for the disaster victim the world has
been transformed from the secure one in which he believed
such things could not happen to one where catastrophe becomes the regular order. In his drastically altered view a
catastrophic universe has come into being. His underlying
feeling may be that the powers that rule the world have
turned against him, have declared their intention to get him,
and, if he has escaped this time, they will try again. However great the destruction in a large-scale disaster, each survivor may have the thought, 'But they didn't get me,' and
then the fear, 'They will come back to finish me off.' This
apprehension is further stimulated by the inevitable feeling
of the survivor in relation to those who succumbed: 'Rather
them than me.' This thought rouses feelings of guilt and the
fear of retaliation: 'What right have I to survive at the expense
of others?'[248]

The fear of recurrence is closely related to delayed reactions to the past event and the tendency to relive it which
we have just discussed. The continued tension and apprehensiveness stimulated by the danger already past is felt as
relating to a new danger to come. The need to gain mastery
over a trauma leads to the wish to repeat it in a less intolerable way.[249] The dreaded repetition may thus be unconsciously wished for. I have spoken of how in reliving the past
event people are preoccupied with what they should have
done which they omitted to do. Similar thoughts are prominent in imaginings about the return of the disaster. In spec-
ulations about the catastrophe to come there is apt to be the
recurrent question: is there something I can do which will
assure immunity? Evidently there is a very real concern to
institute precautions against a hazard of which one has become so vividly and painfully aware. The effort to think of
protective devices is consciously aimed at physical safety.
However, there is also the less conscious question: can I the
next time successfully ward off the feeling of being over-

whelmed and helpless? Dissatisfaction with possible precautions may express not only doubts about their physical efficacy, but also a persisting uncertainty whether one could escape intense feelings of distress in case of another catastrophe. These anxieties often seem related as much to the past as to the future. Thus the frequent inability to imagine some sure protection against another disaster expresses the sense of still feeling overwhelmed by the last.

Apprehensiveness about a new disaster is probably greater to the extent that people were unprepared for the past one. As a tornado victim says, "It does upset you to see a cloud after being just missed, misjudging one like we did, you know, thinking it was a rain cloud and then get caught like that. Well, it does make you jittery."[250] Having been unwary before, people tend to be on the alert and watchful, not to be taken by surprise another time. "Now when a cloud comes up we won't go to sleep, not any of us, unless we know that one of us is watching the cloud, if it's bad."[251] And another tornado victim says, "Frankly, I think I'll know the next time I see a tornado. I don't believe that anybody could ever make me forget that million jets that were roaring up there in that cloud. That's just the way it sounded absolutely. And I didn't have enough sense to know it was a tornado."[252]

The ideal of oneself as one who knows what's up and is ready to cope with it has suffered a blow from one's having been fooled. (This, as I have suggested before, may be particularly important for Americans.) There is also the wish to undo the trauma of sudden terror by going over the same thing but this time with one's eyes open. If it were to happen again one would do the right things and it would not be so terrible. The young couple whose trailer was blown away just after they had left it were told afterwards that, if they had looked back as they turned the corner of the street, they could have seen it happen. As it was, they did not even know till later that a tornado had struck and suffered a shock at the thought of a danger so narrowly missed of which they had not even been aware. On a subsequent occasion when there is a threat of another tornado, and they start driving away from the storm, they do not omit to look back. "This time we were looking back to see what was happening. We were keeping our eyes open to see if we could see one (a tornado) coming or not."[253] Here, as the situation is repeated, there is a making up for the past omission. This time one is doing it the right way. Intense watchfulness replaces the past unwariness. At least one will avoid the shock of surprise, of being threatened by a danger of which one is not even aware, and which for this reason seems the more frightening afterwards.

On a deeper level it may be felt that, in having ignored the signs and warnings of the disaster on the past occasion, one was failing to take seriously the threats of the punishing powers. One laughed off the tornado warnings, saying, 'It can't happen here.' But the powers were in earnest; the blow fell. One then realizes how wrong one was not to have paid attention to the warnings—like a too confident child who did not believe his parents would go through with a threatened punishment. One then attempts to undo this lack of piety by the most sensitive responsiveness to any renewed threat, as if to say to the angry powers: 'I am humble and apprehensive before you. I know very well the awe that is due you. See, I do not laugh. No, I am trembling.' And in response to these signs of submission, perhaps the powers will be content only to threaten, and will not proceed to the full rigors of repeated punishment.

Thoughts of what to do if the disaster recurred often follow the pattern of imagining one or another means of protection and then being beset by doubts about it. The attempt to imagine a situation of immunity is unsuccessful. The feeling of having been helplessly exposed in the past disaster persists. A woman says that if she were to stay in the tornado-stricken town, "I'd build me a concrete cellar and every time it looked like it was half-way gonna storm, I'd get in it. But I don't want to get in some old pole pen and get bit by a rattle snake." Thus the idea of security in a storm cellar is succeeded by that of another danger. She goes on to give advice on the basis of her past experience, and what she did wrong: "Don't get in the corner of the building next to where the wind is coming from. If we had been in our own hallway over the furnace or in the bathroom, there wouldn't have been a hair knocked off us. But we didn't. . . Always get near the center of the building, 'cause it generally takes the main part out and throws it this way. Well, if the wall caves in a little, you'd be in the center, well, you are not apt to get much of it. Or you might get killed, but you stand a better bet."[254] Here again efforts to think of a really safe position end with the breakthrough of the apprehension of irresistible danger: "you might get killed" in spite of all these precautions.

A man tells of his unsuccessful attempt to think of some place where one would be safe in case of another tornado: "I tried to figure out what would be the best, the most secure place to get in a case like this. I thought of a bathtub. . . I just drove around town and think now, in case something like this happened again, maybe we can see something that would help to know what to do if it happened again. Bathtubs? No, I see bathtubs that—homes the bathtubs have gone away and you couldn't even find the bathtub. Well, that's not the safest place after all, and so I don't know."[256] A woman who has abandoned the attempt to imagine a situation of immunity in case the disaster recurs says quite simply: "As far as trying to protect themselves, I don't feel that I know anything to tell anyone, because people were killed in all different circumstances here, outside and inside, in cars and out of cars. So, as far as feeling secure anywhere, I wouldn't, in a cyclone."[257]

This failure to find an insurance against future danger expresses in part the fact that the effort to rectify the past experience, by imagining how one could do it over again, has not succeeded in eliminating the alarm still felt about the hazards undergone. Also there are probably some scruples which interfere with the wish to imagine oneself in possession of complete immunity. Stories like that of *Appointment in Samara* reflect the conviction that man in his pride should not think he can outwit fate. The legend of the Tower of Babel similarly warns against trying to make oneself immune against the recurrence of a catastrophe. I shall speak of this more when I come to the point of how rarely people try to get away from the place where a disaster has occurred. Then there is the sense of guilt, which we have noted before, about having survived where others perished. It may seem presumptuous and unjust to try to claim yet again the prerogative of survival. Rather one says, as it were, placatingly to the resentful dead: 'Look, next time it may very well be my turn.' Again, if one has suffered a serious loss in the disaster, such as the death of a member of the family, thoughts of what one might have done differently can be very tormenting. The achievement of resignation is facilitated by feeling there was nothing one could have done to prevent the fatality.

Anxiety at separation from loved persons is often intensified following a disaster. This is related to the sense of abandonment during impact, for which one seeks subsequent reassurance, as well as to the fear of recurrence: something might happen while the loved ones are away. One's anxiety about their fate at the time of extreme danger persists after the event; or, where such anxiety was inhibited at the time, it emerges later as a delayed reaction. The recent danger situation also tends to revive earlier ones. In early childhood one has felt apprehensive when mother was not there. The little child may fear all kinds of dangers in bed alone in the dark, but these are dissipated when mother comes; when he hears her voice the room even seems less dark. Following a disaster both adults and children may fall back on this early means of reassurance against fear.[258] When they are together with those they love they are less afraid. A mother tells how after the tornado her little girl was afraid to sleep in a room alone: "We had to put her in the bed back in the room with us. She was scared. She said the walls were fixing to fall in on her."[259] Other mothers tell how their children do not want to play outdoors any more; they want to stay in the house close to mother.[260] Similarly wives may become apprehensive when their husbands are away. A man who has to travel in connection with his business relates that when he leaves home, "she (his wife) usually throws a tizzy about it. I don't think I could get too far off without taking her with me."[261]

A woman tells how alarmed she becomes when a storm is threatening and her husband is away; by herself she feels she cannot assess the danger and is inclined to fear the worst. "I guess if my husband was at home and used his judgment on the clouds a little bit I wouldn't be quite this scared... If he was here and let him look at them with me, I'd have somebody else's opinion on it. It would help."[262] Presumably the clouds would seem less threatening if she looked at them with her husband close beside her. A first grade teacher in San Angelo tells of the poor attendance of children at school in the year following the tornado, though normal living conditions had been reestablished: "I have had more people absent this year than I have had in the last ten years... But I attribute it to the diseases we have had. We have had measles and mumps and chicken pox and scarlet fever and pink eye. I have never had so many diseases in one year. And I think the people who were absent were absent because of that more than because of the other (i.e. storm scares)."[263] One might speculate here (and it is something which evidently would have to be checked by more detailed observations) that the susceptibility of these children to diseases was facilitated in this period following the disaster by their fears of leaving home and their longing to stay close to mother.

While a disaster often rouses fears of its recurrence, as we have seen, it is also possible for it to have the opposite effect. Some individuals may feel that having undergone the extreme danger they have, as it were, made payment in full of their debts to the powers that be. They are now in the clear: one cannot be tried twice for the same crime. Or, to take another juridical analogy, if in the hanging of a condemned man the rope breaks, he cannot be hanged a second time. Where those who fear further catastrophes seem to feel that the powers have declared the intention to pursue them to the end, those who feel nothing more will happen seem to assume that the powers have shot their bolt. In other terms, one sacrifice (that of the danger undergone) serves to buy immunity to further hazards. Having survived the disaster one may feel the sense of confidence in one's own invulnerability strengthened. A captain of a British merchant marine ship during the last war, whose ship had been torpedoed but repaired and put back into service, had a piece of the torpedo, which had been removed from the hull, mounted and hung in the ship's lounge. As he proudly displayed this trophy to his passengers, it seemed to be, for both him and them, a talisman of safety. The ship had already undergone the feared danger; it would not happen again.[264]

These alternatives of expecting further catastrophes or feeling that one has gained immunity are evidently related to the subjective near- and remote-miss reactions which we discussed in connection with impact. For the individual who has had his illusion of invulnerability shattered in undergoing the disaster there is apt to be an apprehension that anything may now happen to him. He feels vulnerable; he has lost confidence in his luck. The sense of helplessness against overpowering forces, which he felt so painfully in the moment of impact, persists. But for the one who retained confidence in his immunity during the worst of the disaster, his survival may serve to confirm his belief that nothing can happen to him.[265] Yet it may not always turn out this way either. The person who felt in impact, 'This is the end of me,' may afterwards experience a great sense of reassurance. He may feel, in effect, as if he died during his ordeal and now is born anew. Having survived death, is he not immortal? On the other hand, the person who maintained a sense that nothing could happen to him in the midst of danger may have been repressing his alarm. He may have a delayed reaction (like that of the rider over Lake Constance) and feel frightened to death thinking back on the hazards so barely escaped. His sense of immunity may thus be shattered in the vivid realization of the danger afterwards, and he may feel entirely vulnerable to future threats.

Actual repetitions of danger situations may also have varying effects. The need to repeat in order to gain mastery over a traumatic experience may be satisfied, particularly if the latter event is not too extreme. One has the chance then to relive the disturbing experience in a more tolerable way. A woman in San Angelo speaks in this sense about a severe and damaging storm, which, however, did not assume the proportions of the disastrous tornado of the year before: "I think it probably releases the tension when you have one and you see your house stood up to it. It shows you, and shows your children, that every one of these storms is not a tornado and will not blow your house down."[266] In this instance a partial repetition of the disaster appears to serve as a reassurance against the fear of a recurrence in full force. For others, however, even a relatively mild recurrence may have a discouraging effect. It seems to confirm the belief in a catastrophic world, the feeling that one is cursed. Thus another woman says about the same damaging storm a year after the tornado: "I almost gave up. I thought, 'Well, what's the use?' I thought maybe we was living in the wrong part of town... It's the third time we've roofed the house and it's been beat in."[267] Where the fear of recurrence may have been waning, a new event which recalls the past disaster may revive the belief in an inevitable series of catastrophes. In the incident where Japanese fishermen suffered from radioactive effects in an American bombing test, and where there followed great alarm about the risks of eating contaminated fish, a Japanese student wrote to a newspaper: "I was horror-stricken when I read the news of the Fukuryu Maru incident. The wretched remembrance of Hiroshima and Nagasaki, which was about to disappear from my memory, revived. And I almost felt that the Japanese are destined to A-bomb disasters."[268]

The manner and timing of repetitions of the danger situation make for people's reacting in different ways. Where there is a regular recurrence of the danger, and precautions against it become part of the habitual round of daily life, there is apt to be a marked reduction of alarm. Thus in England during the Blitz, for many Londoners the bombing hazard receded to the status of common dangers to which one gives little thought, such as the risk of crossing a busy thoroughfare.[269] Intermissions in a danger to whose presence one has become habituated make for a revival of apprehensiveness. If one has time to become accustomed to a safer environment, one is again more sensitive to the danger when it recurs.[270] If one has undergone a severely alarming experience, such as that of being in a house that was bombed, one requires some time to recover; otherwise a repetition of the event will be harder to tolerate than the initial experience.[271] This follows from what has been said about the work of mastering a traumatic experience after it is over. If another disastrous event overtakes the individual while the work of mastering the preceeding trauma is still uncompleted, it is evident that his emotional resources will be overtaxed.

There are great individual differences, as already suggested, in reacting to repeated painful experiences. Some individuals seem to learn how "to take it." The memory of past misfortunes which one was able to surmount gives one assurance of being able to recover from new ones. As a woman from San Angelo says about the tornadoes which she has been through at different times in her life: "I was in one of them when I was five and I got over that one. I was in one when I was twelve and I got over that one. And I was in one when I was forty-three and I'm sure I'll get over it."[272] In contrast to such facility for recuperation, there are instances were recurrent misfortunes have a cumulative effect. It would seem that in such cases the individual has been unable to master earlier traumas. He cannot, like the woman from San Angelo, take heart from the recollection of old hardships over which he has triumphed. Rather, a new disaster revives all his unresolved distress about old misfortunes. He sees himself as perpetually beaten down and victimized by fate, and he feels: 'I am the sort of person to whom such things always happen; I am an unloved stepchild of fortune.' Among the many factors which may contribute to such a reaction, we may note: a background of early traumas, which occurred before the individual had adequate means of coping with them; an exceptionally high demand for supplies of love and signs of favor from the environment, predisposing to easy disappointment and to feeling depressed —despised, unloved, and worthless—when things go against him; and masochistic tendencies to cling to and maximize disappointments, which are an unconscious source of gratification.

3.
The place where it happened

╲╱╲╱╲╱╲╱╲╱╲╱╲╱╲╱╲╱╲╱╲╱╲╱╲╱╲╱╲╱╲╱╲╱╲╱╲╱╲

THERE ARE TWO THINGS which are particularly striking in the way people react to the place where a disaster has occurred. People from nearby, who have not been directly affected, tend to feel a strong urge to go to see the place where it happened. Those who have been hit by the disaster, instead of feeling an aversion for the spot, are most often impelled to reestablish themselves on the same ground after it has been built up again.

The influx of great numbers of "sightseers" into a disaster-stricken area, sometimes to the extent of impeding rescue activities, has been repeatedly observed.[273] There are many motives which may be involved in this wish to look at scenes of death and destruction. In our age of combined cruelty and squeamishness, where so many atrocities have been accomplished out of the public view, we may be disinclined to recognize the existence of an urge to look at bloody sights. Executions are no longer a public spectacle, and it would seem strange for a contemporary aesthetician to say, as Edmund Burke did in his essay *On the Sublime and Beautiful,* that a dramatic tragedy, in which the protagonists are only killed in play, can never equal in emotional impact the scene of a public hanging. We have set up certain conditions

(163)

for vicarious participation in such events, mainly by making contact with them more indirect. An execution is not seen by the public but only described in the press. From scenes of war and riot newspapers and magazines bring photographs of dead and wounded. By interposing the media of words and photographs we defend ourselves against the uneasy feelings which would be aroused by a closer inspection.

The urge to look at scenes of violent death is opposed by the feeling that it is something forbidden. In Plato we find an account of a soldier who, unable to resist the impulse to look at a heap of corpses, addressed his own eyes, saying, "There, you wretches, look your fill!" After a plane crash in Elizabeth, New Jersey, a man reported, "One woman had come for miles to see the bodies. Women were competing for places of vantage. It made me ashamed to be a member of the human race." The same man later took photographs of the wreckage.[274] A young man from Waco, Texas, remarked that following the tornado, "I was kinda morbid just to see what happened."[275]

The feeling of the forbiddenness of such looking relates to the sadistic impulses which it vicariously gratifies. The urge to look and uneasiness about looking may also derive from early childhood curiosity. The two great secrets of the adults, from which children feel excluded, are sex and death; and the two seem often closely related in the child's fantasy of sadistic intercourse. Particularly where terrible things, such as bombing raids, occur at night, this may be one of the unconscious associations.[276] The scruples against seeing the dead may also be related to apprehensions that death may be magically contagious or that one may be stricken down by the resentful dead. Some of those who feel impelled to come into a disaster area to look subsequently assuage their guilt by working in rescue activities. They may then condemn others who only come to look.[277]

Many of the sightseers who come into a stricken area may simply veil from themselves the fact that the interest of the scene derives from its association with sudden and violent death. They do not see the corpses, only the material wreckage. All that they consciously feel is that they are curious to see something like that. Warding off any vivid awareness of human loss, they achieve freedom from scruple by the blandness of their reaction. They may also gain reassurance in this way for sympathetic alarm, warding off the apprehension of a danger which might threaten themselves. Since they can view the site of the disaster with little emotion, they can feel that nothing very terrible has happened.

In looking at a scene of devastation in which others lost their lives, the survivor who has shared the danger may celebrate his own escape, his triumph in still being alive.[278] Certain factors are particularly operative in a situation of continued hazard, as in a city undergoing bombing raids. There the sight of damaged areas may serve as an inoculation against sudden trauma. One sees and knows what it is like, in case it should happen to oneself.[279] For those who have been hit by the disaster a survey of the stricken area may help in the work of mastering the trauma, in substituting exact observations for bewildering impressions and terrifying fantasies.[280]

On the part of the disaster-stricken population there may be, understandably, some resentment against the sightseers who come to stare at their devastated homes and to question them about their losses. "All these sightseers and people with their cameras and these souvenir hunters... I got pretty fed up with it. I guess it's just human nature for people to be curious, but still when you're the victim it's not too funny."[281] "I began to think that these people should stay out—those that told me they came in just to see. I resented their presence in other words. The questions they would ask would irritate you just a little bit. I didn't say it, but you wanted to tell them to go on and mind their own business... It was the continuous questioning. A group would come up and ask you questions about your house and your family. Well, he would no sooner leave and you'd look around and there'd be somebody else looking, ready to ask you a bunch of questions."[282]

The satisfaction of looking at scenes of devastation depends to a considerable extent on the spectator's being relatively uninvolved and on his coming to look voluntarily rather than having terrible sights thrust upon him. It also depends on things having been already cleaned up a bit, the bodies of the dead and injured having been removed, so that while one's interest is stimulated by the fact that one is seeing a place of sudden death, one is spared the sight of the corpses. In the absence of these mitigating conditions, the sights of a severely devastated place are apt to be extremely painful. Thus the survivors of Hiroshima and Nagasaki said afterwards that the most terrible part of their experience was the sight of the dead and injured.[283] The inspection of the results of destruction is more apt to contribute to a sense of mastery over terrifying things where the exposure is voluntary, the stimuli not too extreme, and where the individual is not rendered intolerant by the oppression of an immediately preceding trauma.

The conflicts over looking at the results of a disaster, and also the difficulties in seeing clearly at the time of impact and immediately afterwards when one looks for loved ones and dreads what one may find, may occasionally lead to emotional disturbances of vision. A woman who was in her car at the moment when the tornado hit speáks of the flying debris which obscured her vision: "Of course you couldn't see anything. It just plastered the car." Immediately afterwards she ran into the school building where her children were to look for them. "The halls were dark of course and you couldn't hardly see... There were children on stretchers, and I was getting as close as I could and peeping down to see if it could have been my boy." Thus she is desperately trying to see and at the same time fearing what she may see. After finding her children unharmed, and starting to drive home, she makes an effort not to look at the signs of devastation along the way, which she sees nevertheless. "I didn't look very—you know, to the side very much. I guess I looked more than I realized." After finding shelter with a relative, she becomes overwhelmed by the recollection of the destruction which she had covertly observed along the road. "Then is when it hit me hardest. I got to remembering what I had seen, and I thought that half the people of Lakeview would be dead." Some (unspecified) time later she develops a disturbance of vision. "I nearly went blind in my left eye. But that was purely nerves I suppose. My left eye, seemed like a couple of weeks, there was just a film over it, and I wanted to rub it all the time."[284] Perhaps this woman's need to rub her eye was an expression in body language of what we often say figuratively about something unexpected: 'I could hardly believe it—I had to rub my eyes.' In her experience of the disaster, not being able to see and trying not to see had played a prominent part. It would seem that she was repeating these experiences in her subsequent disturbance of vision.

To turn now to the subject of people's feelings about remaining in a disaster-stricken spot, it seems evident that, while some are apprehensive about it, the preponderant preference is to move back in.[285] This has been observed in both wartime and peacetime disasters. People who had been evacuated from London during the bombing raids were already returning in considerable numbers before the war's end. In western Germany, following the war, there was a strong tendency for bombed out city dwellers to return to their old homes, to want to live again in the same neighborhood, if possible in the same block.[286] The survivors of Hiroshima and Nagasaki in large part moved back into the destroyed cities and rebuilt them.[287] In America, people from towns devastated by tornadoes have been mainly inclined to build themselves new homes where the old ones had stood.[288]

There are, of course, material considerations which are relevant here, such as ownership of land and business involvements. However, it is doubtful whether these would necessarily be decisive, particularly in America, for instance, where moving from one town to another is otherwise so frequent. There are, besides, some people who do move away from the place where a disaster has struck; there is no evidence that this is conditioned by their having greater material facilities than those who remain. In those who return to a place from which they have been dislodged by a catastrophe there appear to be certain emotional factors operative in addition to material convenience.

Evidently there are strong attachments to a place which has been one's home. It is easier to break such bonds by a voluntary decision than to have them brusquely severed by circumstances beyond one's control. A woman speaks of her home which has been rebuilt on the spot where the previous one had been destroyed by a tornado: "We had friends that tried to get us not to rebuild on this lot. I said, 'Yes, sir, that's home to me and I'm going to build right here.' "[289] Moreover, the need for restitution following a disaster, for undoing the harm done, for restoring the *status quo ante* so that one can feel (almost) as if it had never happened finds satisfaction in reestablishing life in the same place.

The impulse to master a trauma by repetition is also operative in the return to the disaster locale. If one can go back into the same situation and experience it in a favorable way, the fears aroused by the catastrophe may be exorcized. Similarly it is often felt that, after one has been in a plane crash, the best thing to do is to fly again as soon as possible. Those who move away from the disaster spot, on the other hand, seem to be the ones who cannot face the pain involved in mastering a trauma through reliving it, but would wish to repress it, to escape from all reminders of it. A woman who wants to move away says: "I guess when we get away from here maybe I can take time out and think about a few things, if I get away from out here instead of seeing things that keep reminding me of what has already passed. Now, I know when we was on our vacation, why I didn't have a worry in the world. It was somewheres different, you know. And I didn't even think about the wind blowing or anything out there. But when I'm here at home I sure do."[290]

Closely related to this intolerance for reminders of a painful experience is the fear of recurrence. A woman who has moved away from a tornado-stricken town says, "I still feel that I would have been uneasy. I said, 'That is a silly way to feel.' But I said, 'Every time a cloud would come up, I believe I would have felt a little more uneasy out there.'

That is a silly way to feel because if it hit anywhere else it probably wouldn't hit out there again. However, they claim that towns do have tornado areas."[291] This woman tries to discount her aversion to the disaster area by some of the same arguments which are frequent among those who remain there. However, in this case they do not seem strong enough to overcome the fear of another disaster in the same place.

The thought frequently occurs that the place stricken by a disaster may have something inauspicious about it, that it is a cursed spot. Such a feeling is understandably reenforced by a recurrence of damaging events. Thus a woman from San Angelo, where a violent storm had struck a year after the tornado, asks: "Do you think there might be something here that draws those things this way?"[292] Another struggles against this idea: "There's never been a tornado here before, right in this one area. However, the wind seems a little higher here than any place. It always has. I don't know whether it's —and there was one hit up on 12th Street the year before, a small one. So I can't see where it would affect this part of town, you know, or hit here any quicker than it would any place else. I do, naturally, feel like maybe if I moved two or three hundred miles away I would feel a little safer maybe. But still the way they've been hitting all around... Of course it (the recent hail storm) hit uptown as bad as it did here I think. But I still felt, well, we're getting a little more than our share. But as long as it wasn't any worse than it was, I didn't let it worry me too much."[293] Here conflicting feelings are expressed about the home locality: it has a good record (no previous tornadoes), but the winds are especially high; other parts of town have been equally hit; a place hundreds of miles away might be safer, but tornadoes have been hitting all over, and so on. She fears that the spot where she is may be peculiarly vulnerable, but tries to ward off this idea.

Those who stay in the disaster-struck area struggle to deny that it is a cursed spot. This seems to be one of the meanings of the repeated characterization of the disaster as "just one of those things": that is, it has no special significance, it was not aimed at this spot by a hostile fate. A woman says, "We

didn't do like some of them. Some of them moved off, and
they's afraid to even live back out here. But it's just something that happened, you know. You can't run from it. It
might hit down the middle of somewhere else next time."[294]
Thus other places are equally vulnerable; there was no aim
or purpose in the disaster having struck this town. Staying
in the same place may thus be defended on naturalistic
grounds: disasters are distributed in a random way; there is
no need to move—this place is no worse than any other. Not
moving may also be justified, implicitly or explicitly, on
supernatural grounds, by the idea that if the disaster was
aimed at its victims it can pursue them anywhere.

In the Old Testament story, after the flood people gathered together to build a tower that would be so high that
they would be safe there from any recurrence of the catastrophe. But the Lord did not allow that tower to be com-
pleted. We find a similar theme in *Appointment in Samara*:
someone journeys in the opposite direction from the place
where it has been foretold he will meet with a fatality, but
death overtakes him on the other road just the same. Such
stories, which are widespread, express the belief that one
cannot escape from the powers that be, and that it is impious
to try.

Many disaster victims express the feeling that wherever
they would go another catastrophe might overtake them.
These statements are often ambiguous, implying the operation of natural or supernatural agencies, or both (the naturalistic version cloaking less conscious feelings about the
pursuing fates). "What's the use of going anywhere else? It
might not be another (tornado) coming through here—there
might be another one through tomorrow. Wherever else you
go, there might be one through the same day you get there.
You don't know where they're going to hit."[295] "You couldn't
tell where one is going to strike. You can't run away from
one. That's a thing that happens. It's just as likely to strike
one place as another. As far as running away from one—
you can't do it."[296] "This is as good a spot as any as far as
Texas is concerned. And if I went to Portland (where she

had lived previously), who knows? One (a tornado) might hit
up there. You never can tell . . . I don't know a land that you
can go to where you might not be bombed off the face of the
map today."[297] "I don't think a feller could better hisself any
by trying to run from them. 'Cause he might just accidentally
run right into one."[298]

In the following statements, the relation to supernatural
powers and the impossibility of eluding them becomes explicit. A man says: "That's silly, running from these clouds."
His sister adds, "I think so too. That's the Lord's business.
If he wants it to hit us, well, it's going to hit us."[299] A similar
attitude is expressed by another disaster victim about trying
to build tornado-proof houses: "I noticed in the paper where
they were advertising tornado-proof building material. I
think that's so silly. . . . There's not anything you can put
up against that. When the Higher Power gets ready to take
things like that, to my opinion they're gone."[300]

In the manoeuvering with the higher powers, which is set
in motion by a disaster, there may be the feeling that it is
safest to throw oneself on their mercy. If one attempts to
make oneself stronger than they, by trying to become invulnerable, this constitutes a sin of pride which is likely to
provoke the powers to administer a further lesson. Thus
renouncing the effort to escape is felt as a form of placating
humility. However, it may also conceal an underlying defiance, as if to say: 'I will not be dislodged from the place I consider mine.' Beneath the humble facade of saying there is no
use in trying to run away, no hiding place, there may be the
stubborn feeling: 'You can't scare me.' Also it may be felt
that by running, by showing one is afraid, one only stimulates one's opponent to renewed attacks.

There may also be the feeling that to abandon one's home
ground when it has been hit by disaster is an act of disloyalty.
We speak of rats deserting a sinking ship. A stricken town
needs its children to restore it. A young man seems to be
expressing this sentiment when he says: "Before the storm,
I was planning on leaving. But now I don't care about it. I
was planning on going north some place this summer just

for a change. But now it seems like I'm going to stay here and see everything built up again, and then after that I may go again. But right now I have no hankering to go anywhere else than stay here and rebuild and settle down."[301] In the case of this young man this motive may have been strengthened by the fact that his father was killed in the tornado. He may have felt then, afterwards, guilty for having wanted to leave his home town, to leave his father, so that his resolve to stay may have been an act of posthumous filial piety.

Thus there are a number of motives and beliefs, any one of which, or any combination of which, may be operative in people's returning to a disaster-stricken spot: property investment, sentimental attachment, the wish to undo the damage, the urge to master the trauma by repetition, the belief in a random distribution of disasters (the chances of another would be the same anywhere else), the appointment in Samara argument, the fear of provoking supernatural powers by trying to outdo them, a defiant refusal to be scared away, and a sense of loyalty to the home ground.

4.
Property as payment for life

DISASTER VICTIMS frequently say that, having escaped with their lives, they do not regret the loss of their property. During impact and immediately after, when the issue of life or death is central, there is apt to be a drastic reduction in the value attached to property.[302] Afterwards, though regret for lost belongings tends to make itself felt increasingly, there is often the feeling that one should not complain about this loss, since one has escaped the greater loss of life itself. Material possessions are felt to be the price paid for life. It is a price which one does not, or should not begrudge. This idea of an exchange of property for life occurs repeatedly. Whenever a disaster victim begins to think regretfully of prized possessions lost or debts incurred in replacing a destroyed home, it seems as though he must remind himself of the boon of life, his own and that of his family, which fate has vouchsafed him. He cannot pursue the complaint about his losses with a clear conscience. Whatever price fate has exacted it is not much in comparison with life itself. If one complains, will not fate turn against one for such ingratitude?

The feeling that property has been exchanged for life and that one is glad to have escaped with this lesser sacrifice is expressed in such statements as the following. "We're thankful. We're not thinking in dollars and cents. We're thankful that we're living."[303] "We weren't worried in the least what we lost. In fact we just, you might say, lost about our life's earnings—savings. But it didn't worry us one bit. We were just happy to have been alive, and to have the children not hurt."[304] "All my mind was on was whether they (his family) was a-living or not. It didn't worry me so much about the destruction or what I lost—didn't affect me a bit in the world. It was just their welfare was just all I was thinking about— whether they was dead or alive."[305] "The children said, 'Mother, the house is gone, our clothes are gone, this is gone, that is gone.' I said, 'Yep, but we got ourselves, and we are all together. That's the main thing to be thankful for. We can get these material things back, but lives you can't.' "[306]

This readiness to exchange all one's material possessions for one's life is most wholehearted in the impact of extreme danger and immediately after escaping from it. Later when regrets emerge for lost belongings, one must rebuke oneself for having such thoughts, and remind oneself anew of what one has got for the price paid. Disaster victims repeatedly manifest this compunction about complaining over their losses, and struggle to maintain an ungrudging attitude. A woman speaks with great sadness of the many things she lost when her house was destroyed by a tornado, from the valuable papers she kept in her sewing machine drawer to a new bedroom suite which had just been delivered. " 'Course naturally I think about the things I lost, you know, things I've had for years and would hardly part from any other way. It was all done so soon, you know, so sudden, and everything got rid of so quick. 'Course it was kinda shocking, you know, to think about it. Then too, and then another thing— I didn't think now what a blessing it was, you know, that we wasn't killed. We was spared and we did have our lives, if we didn't have material things. We did have our lives, you see. That is something to be thankful for, of course, more so than material things."[307] Thus she seems to feel guilty about her complaints over material losses and must remind

herself not to begrudge the sacrifice exacted in exchange
for the boon of life.

Others manifest a similar struggle against regret for lost
possessions. " 'Course I was awfully thankful that the family
was all right, you know. There was none of us hurt. Of
course it hurt me awful bad to think that our home was
gone, because we had been ten years accumulating enough
to buy us a home to have to raise our children in. And we
didn't have a fine home, but we were awfully proud of it.
And it hurt mighty bad to think that it was gone. . . . To
see it all go in a minute or two—well, it is mighty hard. But
everybody would say, 'Oh, don't worry about that. Just be
thankful you have your family left.' Well, of course there
was people that didn't have their families, and I was thankful. But still you can't help being hurt when you have lost
your home."[308] This woman seems to feel that she must
justify herself for feeling as strongly as she does about the
loss of her home. Another woman, who has told how she
cried when she found her house gone and came on bits and
pieces of her wedding presents in the mud, struggles to rise
above these regrets, saying: "It leaves you with a sense that
material things are not everything in life. Even though you
might treasure them, though they might make life easier
and living a lot easier, but they're not everything in life.
Because, you know, you could have all the wealth in the
world, without life itself it would be no good."[309]

People who are in a house at the time it is destroyed tend
to feel less grief for its loss than people who are away from
home when the disaster strikes and come back to find their
possessions gone. Evidently if one has undergone a more
acute threat to life itself, one is more ready to make the
sacrifice of material things in exchange for survival. As one
woman puts it: "If we hadn't been in it (the house that was
destroyed) and come home and found all that damage, it
might be it would affect us differently. But after going
through anything like that and get out without being hurt,
you'd be thankful that you're here. You just don't care

whether you have anything or not."[310] In contrast to this, people who were away from home when the disaster struck, and who came back to find their homes destroyed, had more difficulty reconciling themselves to the loss of their belongings, though they also tried to persuade themselves that it was a small price to pay for life. In imagining the circumstances afterwards they felt that they had had a narrow escape. But for them the first shock was the loss of home and possessions. As one woman says about coming home and finding that her house had blown away: "That's a very desolate feeling to know you haven't anything left except what you have on your back." And her husband adds, "Of course we were very thankful in a way that we were alive. . . . But it kinda gives you quite an empty feeling there just going around. Didn't have the heart to pick up some of the stuff that was there."[311] Thus they make an effort to be grateful for survival, not to begrudge the loss of their belongings, but the mood is much more disheartened than in the case of those who experienced a more direct threat to life.

Also in certain kinds of catastrophe belongings may assume an inimical quality. The meaning of a roof over one's head becomes radically changed when one fears that the roof will fall in on oneself and one's children. This was one of the most frequent fears of tornado victims in the moment of impact.[312] Bright, shiny window panes are transformed into dangerous splinters of glass, cherished pieces of furniture may topple and crush their owners. It is perhaps this experience of material things turning inimical which also helps those who are in their houses at the moment of destruction to part with their belongings with less regret. In normal times a house gives a sense of comfort and protection; in the feelings it evokes, it may be compared to a good mother. In a disaster the house may turn into a bad mother who threatens to crush her children.

With the passage of time regret for lost belongings increases. This is partly related to the fact that immediately after the disaster many people find refuge in unfamiliar houses. It is a bit like when one is traveling; one does not miss the many things which one has left at home. However, when households begin to be reconstituted, people expect to find ready to hand all their usual equipment. They then feel the loss of each thing which is missing. As one man says, "Until you start setting up housekeeping again you really don't know what you've lost."[313] And a woman says about her daily life in her newly constituted home: "Now and then, about my household duties, I don't know, you miss the things you had, and once in a while you can't help feel tears come to your eyes."[314]

The passage of time also tends to bring a shift in attitude towards the event. Immediately afterwards one is occupied with thoughts of how much worse it could have been and with feelings of relief for having escaped. In this phase gratitude predominates and there may be moments of elation. As the effect of the extreme threat diminishes, one becomes aware of how much worse off one is than before. The frame of reference, or basis for comparison shifts. One's situation at first seems fortunate, in comparison with the worst that could have happened. Later this image of the worst fades out, and one comes around to thinking of what one has lost in comparison with what one had. This contributes not only to increased regret over property losses but to the general feeling of let-down some time after a disaster has passed. The elevated and generous feelings of the time immediately following, which I shall describe in more detail presently, tend to peter out.

As we have seen, in some disaster victims there seems to be a genuine willingness to part with material possessions which are felt to be the price of life, while others have to struggle with themselves to achieve this attitude. What seems to be commonly felt is that under the circumstances one ought to be ready to part with possessions without complaint. In other words, this is an ideal, more or less approximated by different individuals. This ideal is supported by Christian tradition. As one woman relates, following a disaster: "Preachers have been saying we should all take a lesson that it don't take very long for your earthly treasures to go. An' just like I said, 'Better to store up some of our treasures in heaven.'. . . It seems like when you go to church on Sunday morning the people are more humble. I think it's taught us a lot not to want earthly things so bad as most of us do, try to have all the luxuries in life. And I think we will all think more about heavenly things from now on. Because we sure can't take it with us. And it sure can go if it's the Lord's will—'course we don't know that it was."[315]

The principle of pledging material wealth as payment for escape from danger is widely exemplified in various forms of sacrifice. In embarking on a dangerous undertaking the believer make make a sacrifice to his god or may vow to make one if he returns safely. It is in this way that wagers with fate differ from racecourse betting or roulette: in the latter the winner gets paid, while in the former if one wins, one pays.[316] Bargains with fate in one form or another appear no doubt among the customs of many cultures. However, there would seem to be certain attitudes towards property which may be distinctively American which contribute to this feeling about dispensing with material things.

Americans are often supposed to care a great deal about money. When attitudes about this are examined more closely, however, it appears that they are more interested in making and spending money than in just holding on to it.[317] To inherit money is less a merit than to be able to make it. According to a tendency of Protestant ethical feeling, prospering materially is an index of being in a state of grace. But this implies a conflict with the older Christian depreciation of material things, as invoked, for instance, by the preachers just cited ("Lay not up for yourselves treasures upon earth," etc.). The conflict may be resolved in being able to lose without complaint the possessions in the gaining of which one has demonstrated one's prowess. In a situation of loss, the older Christian attitude towards material things is available to fall back upon.

There is a very general American feeling that belongings are replaceable. There is no sense of loss at parting with last year's car which is replaced by a better model. The same often applies to one's house, one's neighborhood, the city where one lives, one's job, and even one's circle of friends. All may be changed, with the prevailing feeling that one will find just as good or better as one moves along. American mobility is closely involved with this sense of easy replaceability. In the case of loss, a background of material plenty supports the confidence that what has been lost can be replaced. Again, as one disaster victim puts it, "If you had a lot, you can start over and perhaps even have more than you lost."[318] Since the sense of one's own adequacy depends on the activity of getting, starting over again is less distressing than where self-esteem depends more on the static condition of having.

William James described the self as being like an onion, from which one could peel away layer after layer until one reached the central self, the first person singular, "I."[319] There is in a way something distinctively American in this conception of the self. For Americans, to a marked degree, property, physical appearance, even personality can be changed without a sense of the self being altered. One does not like one's appearance: one goes to a charm school and has it changed. One is dissatisfied with one's personality: depending on one's persuasion, one takes a course in how to win friends, or goes to a psychoanalyst. One's idiosyncrasies do not seem essential to one's self. One's mind and body are raw materials which one may hope to work into more ideal forms. All the less are material belongings essential to the feeling of continued personal integrity. In a more traditional culture, the loss of an hereditary estate may make an individual feel that he is no longer the same person. For Americans, who in each generation acquire on their own their major possessions, and, as has been remarked, continue to replace them repeatedly, there is no such involvement of particular belongings with the sense of self.

There is a measure of protection against the possibility of feeling damaged in defining the self in this spare way. The more belongings are included in the definition of the self the more vulnerable one is to losing parts of oneself.

To the extent that belongings are replaceable appurtenances which do not enter into the composition of the essential self, one is more insured against the feeling of being damaged or depleted in losing them.

There is also a strong American feeling against acknowledging that one is in a disadvantaged position. I shall say more about this presently. This also contributes to the curtailment of complaints about losses.

Since we do not have comparative material about reactions to material loss in disaster, we cannot estimate how much these American traits (which, of course, are also affirmed only hypothetically) are significant for the feeling that one should part with property gladly in such circumstances. Evidently there is a very widespread feeling that material goods may be exacted by fate as a payment for life. If the attitudes which I have suggested to be distinctively American also operate, they would strengthen the readiness to sacrifice property without complaint and with less real sense of loss than there may be in other cultures in the same exigencies.

A haunting doubt whether property may not be overestimated is suggested by the stock phrase attributed to hold-up men and known to every little boy who plays with a toy gun: "Your money or your life." The joke which supposedly got the longest laugh ever recorded on radio or television was the following of Jack Benny's. A hold-up man demands: "Your money or your life." There follows a considerable pause, after which Benny says, "I'm thinking it over." The response to such a joke expresses in part the audience's greater readiness to part with their money in comparison with the comedian. There would seem to be mixed feelings about material possessions, the high evaluation of which is opposed by an undercurrent of wondering whether they are really so important. While a disaster imposes the feeling that a sacrifice is required, the conjuring up in fantasy of being faced with the alternative "your money or your life" would seem to express a wish to imagine circumstances under which one would gladly dispense with all one owned.

5.
We were lucky

ONE OF THE most recurrent themes of disaster victims is: "We were lucky." Whatever they may have lost, they stress how much worse it could have been and how much more someone else has suffered.[320] This insistence on having been lucky is, again, perhaps distinctively American. Americans, as I have indicated earlier, have a strong aversion against putting themselves in a dependent or helpless position. Even to appear in any way at a disadvantage is painful. One should be able to feel at all times that one is in at least as good shape as the next fellow.[321] To present oneself as suffering, as an object for pity, is evidently to admit that one is less well off than others or even to seem to be appealing for help. This is incompatible with self-esteem. The preferred attitude is: no one needs to feel sorry for me—I'm all right. The term "sympathy" is often equated with "pity." One wards off the sympathy of others, which implies that one is unfortunate, as if it were an offense.

Americans, as I have also mentioned before, dislike any emotion that has an admixture of pain. Lamenting over one's losses and having others lament with one offers to members of some cultures a measure of gratification. But such emotional outpouring is apt to be disparaged by Americans. They prefer to deny loss, to suppress grief, to curtail mourning.[322] For others, as for instance in traditional Jewish culture, suffering may be compatible with the preservation of their essential relation with their deity. For all their sufferings, the Jews remained none the less the chosen people of their God. His chastening of them was a manifestation of his paternal concern. For Americans it is only by prospering that one can feel that one is not cast out by the powers that be. We shall see presently how they ward off the idea that a disaster is a divine punishment, and rather see God's role in it as that of having saved them from natural hazards for which He was not responsible.

A woman who lost her house and all her belongings in a tornado says, "We was very fortunate because there was lots of people that didn't have a place (to stay for the night). An' we were lucky in havin' a place to go after the storm."[323] Thus one stresses what one has rather than what one lacks, and compares oneself with others who are worse off. A woman in a family where some were injured and where there was much property loss, but no one was killed, says: "I guess we were the most fortunate family in all Judsonia."[324] A woman whose mother was killed and whose home was destroyed says: "I can see where I've got a lot to be thankful for. Even though my home and everything we had was destroyed, and I lost my mother, I can realize we still got a lot to be thankful for, because there was a lot of us in the family—we could have lost more than just one."[325] A woman whose grandson, the only child of her daughter, was killed says, "We were luckier than some who lost two or three out of the same family—and not a stitch of clothes left." She stresses that her family saved some of their clothes, and "I just wished everybody else in that line came out of it as nice as we did—to have a change of clothes anyway."[326]

In effect: we were lucky. We may have lost all our belongings, but we have our lives. We may have lost a member of the family, but we might have lost more than one. We lost our home, but we're lucky to have found a refuge for the

night. I lost my grandchild, but we're lucky to have saved
some of our clothes. There were others who were worse off.
Others lost more than we did. The emphasis is not on what
one lost but on what one has. The basis for comparison is
how much worse it might have been and how much worse
off others are. One cannot help feeling here a strenuous and
even strained defense against acknowledgment of loss. One
feels impelled to ask: Is it not sad to lose one's mother? Is
it not tragic to lose one's grandchild? Is one really so lucky?
I think we see here the extremity of the American denial of
misfortune and inhibition of grief. The woman whose grandchild was killed tells about her daughter, the boy's mother:
"That daughter of mine, she never complained, she never
cried. . . . She said, 'Mother I've done all I can for Billy and
now we are going to try to do something for you.' She never
flinched a time."[327] One does not mourn; one gets on with the
work that has to be done. Of course, this stoical restraint of
grief, like the calm allegedly maintained in moments of danger, represents an ideal which may be more or less approximated in actual behavior. When people proudly claim for
themselves and those close to them such complete mastery
over distressing feelings, we may be justified in not taking
what they say quite literally. What they are expressing, however, is the very high demand which they make on themselves not to give way to fear or grief.

The comparison of oneself with others who were harder
hit is recurrent. A woman whose house was destroyed says:
" 'Course, now, we didn't lose near as much as a lot of people.
We were just lucky there."[328] Another woman, who was able
to salvage some of her household equipment, says: "All in all,
we came out a whole lot luckier than most people. Some
people—the lady over there couldn't even find a part of her
frigidaire or her stove. They were just wiped out. But now
our things weren't that way. We still have the frigidaire . . .
And our electric stove, it didn't have a scratch on it."[329] Another woman speaks of one who lost husband, child, and
home and who takes it very bravely: "It's things like that
that have helped people so much to bear the little things

compared to hers."[330] There is the feeling that one does not have "the right" to complain if others have suffered so much more.[331] Their claims to sympathy are greater than one's own. This is felt the more readily since one does not want to be an object of commiseration in any case. The woman who lost her mother and her home says that when she is tempted to think about these things, "I try to think of something else as much as I can. I think about other people and what they've lost so I don't have time to feel sorry for myself."[332]

As one does not want to feel that one is pitiable, one diverts one's pity to others. It is the same mechanism which we noted earlier by which people maintained their sense of being able and active by pointing to others who needed help more than they did. In this way one wards off the feeling of being at a disadvantage and the possibility of being in a dependent position.

It is felt to be shameful to have others feeling sorry for you, and particularly inadmissible to seem to ask for sympathy. As one disaster victim puts it, " 'Course, I don't believe in going around and telling all our troubles and all our sorrows and heartaches and advertising for — you know — for sympathy. I don't believe in that."[333] Another says: "I don't like to tell our troubles to anybody, and if I do I want to make it funny. If it even was serious, I think I would rather see you laugh over it. I don't think I want anybody's sympathy is the main thing. And I'm the sort of person that will not say anything to get it."[334] It is felt to be an imposition on others to expose them to anything which could arouse painful feelings. If one tells about ordeals one has undergone one may, as this woman does, try to make a humorous story of it. An economy of painful emotion is thus achieved for both the others and oneself. One does not want to be a gloomy or complaining person whose company would not be pleasant. And pity, which would be an offense to one's self-esteem, is warded off. It is a matter of pride not to ask for anything. But to tell with real sadness about misfortunes one has suffered is to ask for sympathy. Instead of falling into such a position of seeming to need something from others, one gives them something, namely, the amusement provided by the humorous story. We shall see later that this attitude of not needing anything from others comes out very strongly in relation to post-disaster relief.

The sympathy of others is also warded off because it is such a potent stimulus for evoking one's own feelings of sadness. A man who stresses how much he maintained emotional control throughout the disaster says: "My emotions more or less got the best of me when so many friends came in. It just made you kind of choke up a little bit, you know. They were feeling sorry for you, or they were sympathizing with you just a little bit and it kind of—you'd see some fellow come up that you had known all your life, or maybe your best friend, and say 'Well, Johnson, I sure am sorry to hear this,' and all that. It would kind of bother you a little bit, but it never did bring tears or anything like that. I didn't sob. The way I did it—I said, 'Well, I'm lucky my folks are alive. The loss (of his house which was destroyed) is nothing compared to what it could have been.' "[335] The wish to avoid emotion is patent in the style of speech: the repetition of the phrase "a little bit," the colorlessness of the expressions used. The feeling of intensified sadness combined with assuagement when a friend expresses genuine sympathy for one's loss becomes: "It would bother you a little bit." The welling up of emotion is a bother; it disturbs the predominant blandness which is felt to be normal and comfortable. The sympathy must be warded off; one does not want even one's best friend to feel sorry for one, because this implies that one is in a damaged condition. Thus expressions of sympathy are countered with: 'I'm lucky, see? No one has to feel sorry for me.'

The circumstances of the disaster are analyzed to demonstrate the relative benevolence of its having struck in just the way it did. It could have been much worse. "If it had hit farther over here, why, you know, it would have killed lots more people ... And if it had waited about fifteen or twenty more minutes all the first grade children would have been out of school. They would have been coming home and it would have killed every one of them, because you couldn't live outside at all because everything was flying."[336]

A disastrous event does not make one see one's life in a tragic perspective. Rather one reminds oneself of the many good things one has had which certainly outweigh the present misfortune. Thus a woman says: "It didn't make us any difference what we had lost. We celebrated our twenty-fifth wedding anniversary on Sunday before it happened on Monday. I felt like we had had years and years of happiness."[337]

If one recalls past hardships it is to remind oneself how one was able to surmount them. One not only feels good about having survived, but confident in one's capacity to cope with difficulties. The goodness of life is not estimated predominantly in terms of benefits received; one does not feel crushed because supplies from without are brusquely reduced. The emphasis is on one's strength and resilience in being able to take things, one's activity and resourcefulness in recouping one's situation. The same woman who spoke of her years of happiness adds, "We had had disasters before in one way or another, not nearly as bad as this, but things do happen to people. We had overcome them. We had been through a depression, and one child had polio. We've had things happen to us and we always seem to get over them. And I felt like we would get out of this."[338] This confidence in one's capacity for recuperation, one's ability to master difficulties is, again, an American ideal. Evidently not everyone can measure up to it, and those who claim to feel this way may be sometimes suppressing more discouraged feelings. However, if one succumbs to misfortune, if one gives way to despair, one's distress is all the greater in the realization that one is not behaving as one should.

However, while one minimizes one's misfortunes, one does not permit others to do so. Even though one brushes sympathy aside, one wants due acknowledgment of what one has been through. This comes out in the indignant rage of one disaster victim when she hears that the Red Cross in another state has misinformed her son, who is living there, about what happened to her. Her whole house was destroyed, and she was bruised and battered, and they have told her son that nothing happened to her. "He went to the Red Cross there in Texas and they told him that I wasn't even in the storm and that my house wasn't even touched. Imagine! Isn't that awful. And that boy thought, you know, that everything was all right . . . When she told him, you know, that I wasn't even bothered, that I wasn't even hurt—was hurt worse than any of them as far as that is concerned. 'Cause wasn't a piece of it left. It was just demolished and everything I had in it."[339] Thus the suppressed sense of the magnitude of the damage one has suffered comes to the surface when someone else fails to acknowledge it. This same woman, in another context, speaks of what a "blessing" it was that she and her younger son, who was at home with her at the time, came through alive; she curtails her complaints and stresses her advantages. But when someone else fails to acknowledge what she has been through, she breaks out with: "I was hurt worse than any of them." We might say that a certain convention is generally observed: one plays down one's own losses; one expects others to give due acknowledgment to them; and one brushes this aside with the assertion of how lucky one is. However, others' acknowledgment, even though one must demur from it, is essential. To say that these are conventions does not, of course, detract from their deeper emotional significance. What we seem to find is a marked ambivalence to the response of others to one's misfortunes. Insofar as this response contains an element of awe and admiration of the extremity of the experience which one has undergone, it is acceptable and even required. But to the extent that this response contains an element of pity, an implication that one is damaged and unfortunate, it must be forcefully repudiated.

Closely related to the feeling of having been lucky is the readiness to start all over again. Instead of brooding about their losses, people turn their minds to rebuilding their homes and getting life reorganized. A man from an Arkansas town that was destroyed by a tornado says: "About the third day some of them began to see the brighter side of it and to talk about, 'Well, I wanted to change the house anyway and now will be an opportunity.' . . . They didn't have their minds so much on the destruction as they did getting started all over again."[340] Thus one refuses to take even a disaster as something going entirely counter to one's wishes. One extricates oneself from the position of a passive sufferer. Like the man quoted, one thinks if one's house has been destroyed: Well, I wanted to change it anyhow. The forced rebuilding is taken as falling in with one's own intentions. With this spirit one is not likely to be wholly frustrated or outdone by fate.

6.
The rise and fall of the post-disaster utopia

FOLLOWING A DISASTER there is apt to be a great upsurge of good will and helpfulness among the survivors and on the part of outsiders who come to their aid. I have already spoken of this in discussing the altruistic feelings which are stimulated by such an event. Those who have undergone the impact of the disaster have in that moment concentrated their emotional energies on themselves. Afterwards there is a compensatory expansion of feelings towards others, partly motivated by the guilt of not having cared what might happen to them when one's own life was in danger. In the moment of impact, as we have seen, the victim is apt to have an illusion that he alone is affected and to suffer painful feelings of being abandoned by others and by fate. The discovery that one did not suffer alone and the sight of friendly hands held out to help one are all the more prized against this background of loneliness. Also, having been chastened by the punishment of the disaster, one is eager to be exceptionally good to make up for past derelictions and to ward off further retribution.

A disaster provides great, even excessive, vicarious satisfaction for the negative component of feelings towards others. This component having been satiated, the positive sector comes into the ascendancy. One feels more purely loving towards other people in the temporary abeyance of negative sentiments. This affects also class and race distinctions, which are in ordinary times supported by readily available resources of hostility. With the depletion of hostility such barriers are apt to drop temporarily; there is a moment of feeling a sense of all-embracing human brotherhood. I have mentioned also how often following a disaster there are false rumors that this one or that one has been killed. When people meet again their fellow-townsmen whom they had thus supposed to be dead, they feel impelled to embrace them in affectionate welcome. The death of even a casual acquaintance arouses some regret; one is naturally overjoyed to see many as it were return from the dead. Again, there is a need to overcome feelings of helplessness following an overpowering experience, which can be satisfied in giving help to others. In this way one can reaffirm one's own intactness and capacity for activity; it is others who are damaged and in need of help and oneself who is strong and able to give aid and comfort.

On the part of those not directly affected there is a tendency to idealize the victims of a disaster. There are two major images which apply here: that of the martyr and that of the hero. The innocent victim falls heir to the role of the martyr. Those who survive often feel in relation to those who succumb: it was him or me—I'm glad it wasn't me. From this there follows an apprehension of the vindictive dead. But this in turn may be warded off by the thought: he died willingly to save me. By this transformation the innocent victim assumes the aura of a saviour. From the point of view of outsiders there is something extremely impressive about those who have passed through a terrible danger and survived, and who are able to carry on with life afterwards. So, for example, an American observer visiting Hiroshima four years after the dropping of the bomb, and seeing the many survivors who had set up life anew in the city rebuilt on its ruins, says: "There are deeper resources of courage and regeneration in human beings than any of the philosophers had dared to dream."[341] This capacity of human beings to survive extreme ordeals partakes of the quality of heroism, in the myths of heroes who survive incredible hazards by force of their superhuman strength and their near-invulnerability. Thus those who have suffered extraordinary assaults, whether they succumb or survive, are apt to seem more noble than ordinary people, and to evoke the admiration and love which are the due of superior beings.

Further, in ordinary life positive impulses towards people are often thwarted, while in extreme situations they find opportunity for expression. In normal times people are suspicious of strangers who approach them; the presumption is that their motives are not benevolent. Strangers who approach each other in a disaster-stricken town are more readily assumed to be helpful and generous in their intentions. Where in ordinary times compassion for the unfortunate is often qualified by doubts whether it is not their own fault, in a disaster the worthiness of the victims is beyond question. So, for example, in England, many who had suffered alone, without sympathy, during the depression, discovered the joys of generous support and friendly assistance during the wartime bombings.[342]

A sense of the goodness and helpfulness of people is frequently expressed by disaster victims. As survivors of recent tornadoes have put it: "I might say it is a heartwarming experience to see how your friends come to your rescue under circumstances like that."[343] "If we hadn't had help, friends and relatives, I don't know what we would have done. Because they all came out, you know, and worked so hard. Oh, they just worked awful hard (to rebuild the house that had been destroyed)."[344] "Friends just mean so much more to you, and at the time it just seemed like everyone loved one another. All the neighbors felt the same way."[345] "I said you sure did feel popular. We were getting so much attention, because everyone we ever knew came to see about you."[346] "Oh, it's been just wonderful. I just didn't know that people did such nice things for other people."[347] "It's made people friendly, a lot more willing to help each other, because it seems like it has brought them closer together, you know."[348]

Similarly one who was present at the great Chicago fire related: "I saw a great many kindly acts done... The poor helped the rich, and the rich helped the poor... There are no strangers here. There are no ceremonies. The cement of kindred sorrow has done its work. Everybody speaks freely to anybody, and even the churl finds his human side and turns it genially towards us."[349]

This emergence of a state of warm fellow-feeling and active and generous mutual aid depends in part on the nature and extent of the disaster. In some disasters, those who are as yet untouched may be impelled to shun the victims as sources of danger to themselves, as, for instance, in plagues and epidemics.[350] Adequacy of aid to the stricken also depends on the resources of people and supplies in the vicinity which have remained undamaged and the availability of the larger environment for purposes of aid. The ratio of uninjured to injured and dead within the community, the destruction or intactness of such crucial resources as hospitals, and the readiness of the surrounding area to provide remedial personnel and supplies, in terms, for instance, of there not being competing claims at the same time—are all relevant. In American peacetime disasters, such as tornadoes, the uninjured have far outnumbered the injured and dead, and have been quick to go into action as rescuers immediately following the event. Remedial personnel and supplies from outside have poured into the stricken area far in excess of what could be used.[351] There is then apt to be a feeling of rapid mastery of difficulties, of willingness to help coupled with effectiveness.

In Nagasaki, by contrast, following the bombing, survivors wandered for days among the ruins, shrinking from the sound of passing planes, without aid from outside, struggling with the excessive tasks of burying their dead, caring for their sick and dying, and trying to salvage the minimum necessities of life. Insofar as any constructive efforts were weak and ineffectual in relation to the overwhelming devastation, these survivors did not feel afterwards that they had experienced a phase of intensified human goodness after the disaster. Rather they reproached themselves for how little they had been able to do for even their own families.[352] This self-reproach may be related to extreme moral demands, the non-fulfillment of which cannot be excused by any extenuating circumstances. However, it also seems possible that the emergence of an atmosphere of great good will and helpfulness may depend to some extent on the adequacy of human and material resources for the work of immediate aid. Where such resources sink below a certain minimum in relation to the amount of the damage, there may be a predominant feeling of discouragement, and of how little people can do for one another, rather than the exalted mood of a post-disaster utopia.

Where a post-disaster utopia has come into being, in the sense of intensified fellow-feeling and generosity in giving aid, it tends to break down as time goes on. Partly, negative feelings towards people recuperate. The love that was felt in a situation of life and death becomes mitigated by reviving annoyances and antagonisms as things return to normal. Those who have volunteered to help find their enthusiasm waning, their tasks becoming a chore, as the atmosphere of an extreme situation becomes dissipated.[353] Some who have given supplies without counting the cost in the time of greatest urgency begin to regret their generosity and to wonder whether they should not be reimbursed.[354] Usual attitudes about giving and taking are reestablished. Habits of independence and self-sufficinecy complicate the acceptance of further aid. Suspicions arise about people who readily accept the help of relief agencies. The lofty feeling of having been lucky to survive and not grudging one's losses begins to give way to doubts whether one has received one's share of remedial aid. Instead of comparing oneself to others who are worse off one begins to look with envy at those who are better off.

The breakdown of the post-disaster utopia is exemplified in the attitudes towards organized relief agencies. Mutual aid on an informal basis in an extreme situation does not compromise one's sense of independence. Thus people who have just lost their homes accept a blanket that someone puts around their shoulders, warm food, and a place for the night gratefully and without constraint. Very soon, however, usual scruples revive about accepting things from others which it is felt should be got by one's own efforts. As soon as formal relief agencies enter on the scene, the feeling is aroused that to accept help from such sources means becoming an object of charity. This, perhaps to a particularly high degree for Americans, is very negative. Speaking of efforts to distribute relief funds, one woman reports: "We found almost 100% people would say, 'Oh, we can get along. Maybe there is someone who needs it worse than we do.' "[355] Another relief worker says, "I got so mad at people because they wouldn't take those groceries (from the Salvation Army). I just begged them to take them. 'Oh, no, somebody may need them worse than I do'—that would be their answer. There's still a lot of people that need help that won't get it."[356] Thus what is felt to be charity is warded off as an offense to one's self-sufficiency.

The recurrent assertion that others need it more does not, however, entail benevolent feelings towards those who take the help which one has oneself refused. In the moment of refusing, people seem to distinguish themselves from the unfortunate who really need help. But when it comes to talking about those who accept "charity," these latter rarely appear to be worthy cases. Rather they are considered as spongers—whether stingy rich or transient hoboes—who want something for nothing. One woman who tells how she spurned the idea of going to eat in a Red Cross kitchen while her house was being rebuilt, says, "There were people here in town who have millions, I should say thousands, who ate every meal on the Red Cross. But they had everything swept away. There were others who hadn't lost anything in the storm, and had everything to do with (i.e. all their household equipment), but they just didn't want to cook, that's all." She tells about a family she has heard of who came to the Red Cross kitchen "and sat down and ate like mad, and they have things at home, stoves and everything to cook with.

He'd just sold a hardware business for a big price. So I know they wasn't broke. I believe they feel they're doing what they shouldn't. They probably say, 'That's what it's there for. Why not get the benefit of it?' But we feel different. If the time comes when I have to take charity, I will, but it's gonna be a have-to case."[357] At the opposite end of the scale from the greedy rich who take what they do not need, but equally condemnable, are those who are indigent through their own shiftlessness. "There's hoboes around here go in and get a meal off them (the Red Cross). 'Course that's the way they make a living anyway."[358] Thus the suspicion is repeatedly voiced that those who take this sort of help either do not need it or do not deserve it. As one wards off the temptation to compromise one's self-sufficiency one feels strong condemnation for those whose standards are less severe.

When people do apply for aid this is apt to involve many negative feelings. It is already humiliating to make such an application. If it is not granted, the resentment is all the stronger because one has undergone this shame for nothing. One woman speaks of her distress at hearing that a committee of her fellow-townsmen had decided against her family's application for a loan from a relief agency: "I was really hurt. We had lived here all our lives. Never needed help but this one time." She seems to feel that she has been treatd with the lack of sympathy appropriate to the habitual beggar, and tries to assuage her chagrin by reiterating that this was the one time her family had deviated from their respectable self-sufficiency. Like other disappointed relief applicants, she stresses the fact that others have received aid who deserved it less: "There were lots of hard feelings (about the relief agency in question). They helped people that were a lot more able to help themselves than we were."[359] There is thus a shift from the immediate post-disaster tendency to congratulate oneself in comparison with others who were worse off to a keen sense of one's lacks and losses in comparison with those who have more advantages in the struggle for recovery.[360]

Immediately after the disaster there is an uncalculating

giving of help to whoever needs it. Feelings of sympathy are stimulated by the amount of loss a family has suffered. There is a marked shift when relief organizations begin to operate in that they give aid not in relation to losses undergone but in relation to the resources which the family still has at its disposal. The longing for compensation proportionate to what was lost is frustrated. The procedures of relief agencies in investigating the circumstances of applicants often arouse resentment. Disaster victims feel that, instead of their losses being acknowledged and giving them a clear right to compensation, they are put in the position of ordinary applicants for charity whose claims are regarded with suspicion. This is expressed in many complaints against the cold and bureaucratic procedures of certain agencies. Others, by contrast, whose members arrived immediately after the disaster, threw brotherly arms around the survivors and gave them coffee, and also subsequent aid without any questions asked, evoked warm appreciation. They participated in the post-disaster utopia which the more bureaucratic agencies seemed to shatter.[361]

Thus immediately following a disaster there is the impulse to give without stint and to accept without constraint. Later, conflicts about accepting help trouble the disaster victims at the same time that sources of aid become less accessible and seem more grudging. Friends, neighbors, volunteers from the next town become absorbed again in their own usual activities and preoccupations. And one is faced instead with a functionary of a relief agency who seems to wonder whether one's application for a loan may not be a bit of swindling. One is torn between one's need for help and one's ideal of self-sufficiency, which makes one resent those who seem to have less scruples about getting aid. At the same time that people feel strong compunction about accepting help they become engaged in a covert or overt competition for it. And resentments are engendered about injustices in the distribution of relief goods and funds. In extreme cases, those who are supposed to distribute the relief are accused of monopolizing it for their own advantage. Thus, in one of the flood-stricken cities in Holland, the upper class ladies in charge of clothes distribution were accused of keeping fur coats for themselves.[362] In a Mexican town that had suffered a severe flood, the mayor was accused of selling relief supplies instead of giving them to the needy.[363]

In contrast to the feelings of gratitude of victims towards those who first come to their aid with such generosity, there is later often the feeling that relief agencies are unduly concerned with getting credit for their work, advertising themselves, and pushing aside competing organizations. There is a competition for the "possession of the disaster."[364] The townspeople feel that their efforts to help each other in the emergency are belittled by agencies that subsequently take charge of organized relief. It sometimes appears that these agencies are also competing with each other. One has established headquarters in a church; another offers to make a contribution to the church if the building will be turned over to them.[365] The earlier atmosphere of lofty altruism becomes dissipated.

But apart from possible injustices in the distribution of relief, or other unfortunate incidents, it seems unavoidable that the post-disaster utopia should decline. The initial good feelings of both the survivors and those who come to their aid from outside are a reaction to an extreme event the impression of which is bound to wear off. Moreover the experience of a disaster may rouse expectations of compensation which it is not possible to gratify. After punishment one may expect a wonderful forgiveness. There are various religious beliefs to the effect that the millennium will be ushered in by mankind passing first through terrible destruction. In the time immediately after the disaster, when generous feelings are in the ascendant, there may be a sense of the millennium having arrived. "It just seemed like everyone loved one another."[366] Does this not suggest the kingdom of heaven, the kingdom of love? We have heard how people embraced acquaintances whom they had supposed dead. We may recall paintings of heaven where the dead who have arisen again embrace one another. To a certain extent this picture of the immediate post-disaster world is one-sided. There are also accounts of ungenerous and unhelpful behavior at this time. But there is an effort to minimize such negative incidents, to maintain the view that everyone was wonderful. The demonstrations of help and good will which the disaster victim receives may conceivably be construed in terms of an anticipated millennium. He overestimates them and is also unprepared for their dwindling away.

As the lofty mood of the moment of extremity becomes dissipated there is apt to be disappointment for those who are still struggling to recover from their losses, and who had felt encouraged, both by their own longings and by the response which they at first received, to expect so much more. Where there are high demands for self-sufficiency, as among Americans, such disappointment is likely to be suppressed or repressed. It comes out indirectly in a reenforcement of the negative images of both those who give (the unfair, bureaucratic, etc., relief agencies) and those who get (the parasites, objects of charity, people without pride). Emerging from the post-disaster utopia in which help was given freely and could be accepted without compunction, the disaster victim resumes his stance of sturdy self-help, but often perhaps with covert feelings of regret.

7.
Relations to the powers that be

FOR MANY PEOPLE today a sense of the omnipresence of the divine, or of any continuous or well codified intercourse with it, is not very vivid. However, we are apt to have certain, implicit, unreflecting, often inconsistent beliefs on this score. Extreme events tend to bring such implicit beliefs to the surface. It is both frightening and offensive to our self-esteem to suppose that our lives can be drastically altered or disposed of altogether by the action of chance and meaningless forces. This feeling of protest against accidental fatality is expressed, for instance, in *The Bridge of San Luis Rey,* where the investigation of the friar aims at showing that the seemingly arbitrary end to the lives of the victims was rather a fitting conclusion to the personal drama of each one of them. The belief in intentional and purposeful causation precedes that of mechanical causation in the child's view of the world.[367] Drastic and disturbing events are likely to re-arouse in the adult these earlier beliefs.

The tendency to feel that there is a human-like intent in a disaster is exemplified in the imagery which those who have suffered it frequently use to describe the experience of its impact. According to a tornado victim, it was "like someone comin' in here all of a sudden an' hit you over the head with a gun."[368] And another says, "I just felt like someone was trying to tear my heart out . . . just like someone had a hold of your heart and was trying to tear it out."[369] Such images suggest that to the victim's way of feeling, the force of the disaster is personified. William James expressed this more explicitly in relation to the San Francisco earthquake: "All whom I consulted on the point agreed. . . 'It expressed intention,' 'It was vicious,' 'It was bent on destruction,' 'It wanted to show its force.' "[370] Thus in the moment of being struck by an overpowering force there seems often to be the feeling of an agency that acts with intent.

When the toll of the disaster is reckoned up afterwards the problem arises for many of those affected how to fit the occurrence of such devastation and loss into their view of the world. The question of why such a thing should have happened comes up repeatedly, and answers in terms of mere physical forces (in the case of a tornado, for instance) often leave a sense of painful puzzlement. Answers are sought rather in terms of a purpose which would give meaning to what has happened, or an agency to which responsibility and blame can be attached. People wonder why some survived and others perished, those who were saved often struggling against feelings of pride and guilt about their good fortune.

For the religious believer a disaster poses again the traditional problem of evil: why does God let such things happen? In terms of blaming the people on whom the disaster has fallen or God for sending it or not preventing it, there are four possible solutions to this question. First, God is good but the people have sinned and he is punishing them. Second, it is not the fault of the people, but the deity on whom they relied for protection has shown himself ineffectual or ill-disposed. In other words, the people are good, but their god is no good. Third, neither God nor the people are to blame. The disaster has occurred from the action of natural forces for which God is not responsible, but from which he has protected people as far as possible. In this view both God and people are good. Fourth, supernatural agencies are malicious, or indifferent, or non-existent, and human nature is depraved. There is no good either in god or man. This is the position of despair.

To consider these alternatives in more detail, primitive idol-worshippers who were said to destroy their idols in times of misfortune expressed the judgment that their gods were no good if they could not do more for them. We find a similar reaction in the person who, confronted with a terrible event, loses his faith, feeling that if such a thing can happen God does not exist. Voltaire was stimulated by the great Lisbon earthquake to write a critique of the belief in a God who arranges everything for the best. In *Candide,* the maxim of the philosopher Pangloss, that "everything happens for the best in this best of all possible worlds," seems patently inappropriate in the context of a sequence of devastating events.

We find an opposite reaction when people blame themselves rather than their gods for the sufferings which they undergo. This tendency has been strongly marked in the Jews, as Freud has pointed out.[371] The misfortunes which befell them did not make them doubt the power and goodness of their God. Rather they brought forth their prophets who told them how they had sinned to deserve such punishment, so that their moral demands upon themselves became progressively more severe and more complicated. It is reported that some eastern European Jewish communities reacted in the same spirit of self-condemnation to the persecutions of the Nazis.[372] As the inhabitants of a town were driven from their homes and were awaiting deportation to concentration and extermination camps, their rabbi spoke to them, saying: We have sinned; we have not kept the dietary laws, we have not lived clean lives, and so our end has come.

I have spoken repeatedly in the foregoing pages about the tendency, here so strongly exemplified, to react to disaster as if it were a punishment. A factor which may strengthen the inclination to react in this way is a belief in communal guilt. The feeling that a whole community is infected by the moral derelictions of some of its members makes for a greater readiness to interpret a comprehensive disaster as a punishment. Where, on the other hand, the belief predominates that each individual is solely responsible for his acts, and that retribution is precisely meted out to each one for his particular misdeeds, a communal disaster may relieve the individual of feelings of guilt. On the basis of such a belief in individual responsibility, a person may feel he is being punished when misfortunes befall him singly. But when he becomes involved in a large-scale disaster he may be more disposed to feel: this cannot be aimed at me.

What may be a distinctively American solution of the problem of evil, in its avoidance of all blame and guilt, in its unshaken confidence that both God and man are good, appears in the statements of some tornado victims. As a woman from Arkansas puts it: "We've had several good preachers that have come in here and talked about the storm and they say no one knows why it was sent on us. They said not to feel like it was sent on us, that it wasn't... I don't think any of us thought that it was sent on us really. I think we just felt like it come and the Lord saved us and protected us. An' I don't think I heard anybody make the statement they felt like it was the work of God. An' I don't feel like it was either, because He certainly did, it looks to me like, give everybody courage to get right up an' start out workin' to start back."[373] Thus the storm was produced by natural causes, and God saved people. Others, subscribing to this view, stress the amount of physical damage from which so many human creatures emerged unscathed. A woman from San Angelo, speaking of how the tornado there had hit the schoolhouse full of children, says: "When you think of the number of children there is in a building like that and you drive up and see it with the windows out and one whole room caved off and portions of the roof caved in, you begin to get a few serious thoughts, I'll tell you. Just don't see how in the world any of them can be protected. Now, I want to tell you, God protected our school children. There wasn't one child you would call seriously injured."[374]

This view of the division of responsibility between natural forces and God seems particularly suited to the distribution of damage caused by such disasters as tornadoes. Material destruction is tremendously greater than human damage. The average yearly toll from tornadoes in the United States over the past fifty years has been two hundred people killed and twenty million dollars worth of property damage.[375] The survivors of tornado-stricken towns see whole neighborhoods leveled to the ground while most of their inhabitants come out alive. These circumstances fit very well with the idea that physical forces lay waste material things while God protects people.

Implicit in this incompletely articulated theological position is the assumption that God is not omnipotent. The storm blows up without His having any say about it. He then does the best He can to see that people suffer as little as possible. God becomes like a doctor whom one does not blame for the occurrence of disease, but to whom one gives credit for mitigating its effects. This conception of a God whose control over things it limited may be particularly congenial to Americans, who do not like the idea of any individual or agency getting too much power.[376] In *The Will to Believe,* William James spoke of a God who needed people's belief in him in order to exist—something like a presidential candidate who needs our votes in order to become president. In any case, as far as the problem of blame for a disaster is concerned, the assumption that God is not omnipotent serves to exonerate both God and man. Since the disaster occurs without divine intent there is no occasion to doubt God's benevolence or to interpret the sufferings of the victims as a punishment.

Most survivors avoid saying or implying that those less fortunate than themselves in any way deserved their fate. One woman from San Angelo, however, does take the view that it was people's own fault if they came to grief, not in the sense of their having led sinful lives, but rather in their being obstinately wrong-headed about what to do in the moment of danger, and particularly in not taking a woman's advice. "It's just nothing but Providence. It wasn't meant for anybody to be killed. Because look at the many funny things that happened out here. Wherever people went, that's what was saved. If people were in the corner, the whole house went except the corner. A mother and daughter were in a closet—the whole house went except the closet. It just wasn't meant for them to be taken. And some that were taken in the storm wouldn't have been taken if they had done right, now. This old man, Mr. Jones, that his name was given first every time among the list, well, he was by the chimney and his daughter begged and pleaded with him to get away from that chimney and he wouldn't do it. When that chimney came down, it came down on him." And speaking of another man, "his wife just begged him to get under the piece of furniture she was under but he just laughed at her, 'Ha, ha, ha, the idea of me a-crawling under nothing! Naw, I'm going to stand right here.' And she kept a-begging and he kept a-laughing and the walls fell in on him and killed him."[377]

A frequent reflection of disaster victims is that it is "just one of those things."[378] Or, "of course, I realize that things like that happen. Nothing you can do about it."[379] In such laconic phrases there is probably compacted an important part of the philosophy of life of the inarticulate people who express themselves in this way. There is an effort here to accommodate oneself to a hard reality. Before the disaster there was the assumption that such things just don't happen, or couldn't happen to me. Afterwards there is the acknowledgment: thinks like that do happen. The generalized form of the statement implies that the disaster that has befallen the individual is not a unique event, but one of a class (one of those things). It is something that happens to others, that could happen to anyone. Thus the particular disaster which one has undergone was not aimed at oneself. There may be a genuine naturalistic view that such events are distributed in a random way or an effort to deny a deeper feeling that the disaster was aimed at its victims as a punishment. A preoccupation with the physical causes of a disaster such as a tornado may be a defense against anthropomorphic fantasies about it. The reflection that there is nothing you can do about it may express an effort to ward off regrets about what

one should have done but omitted to do, in the way of pre-
disaster precautions or of the better life one should have led
which might have prevented one's being visited with catastrophe. Thus the characterization of the disaster as "just one
of those things" may imply a denial of the victims' guilt and
of the misfortunes they have suffered being a punishment.
"It's just one of those things" appears as a secular counterpart to the statement: God did not send it against us.

How difficult it is to avoid the idea of punishment is shown
by the fact that the same people who deny that the disaster
was "sent on us" nevertheless take it as a "lesson." The woman
from Arkansas whom I quoted before says that, according
to the preachers, "We should all take a lesson that it don't
take long for your earthly treasures to go. . . I think it's
taught us a lot not to want earthly things so bad as most of
us do, trying to have all the luxuries in life. And I think we
will think more about heavenly things from now on."[380] But
what kind of a lesson is it that must be learned by means of
such severe inflictions? The idea of such a lesson comes very
close to that of punishment. Severe parents in punishing
their children frequently say that this will teach them a lesson; or they may say, "This will teach you," as a kind of
euphemism for the punitive act. "I'm going to teach you a
lesson," in this context, may be a self-righteous way of saying,
"I'm going to lick the living daylights out of you." The
woman who spoke of having learned the lesson not to want
earthly things so much adds: "We sure can't take it with us.
And it sure can go if it's the Lord's will. 'Course we don't
know that it was." Thus the thought breaks through that
there was a divine intent behind the deprivations suffered
by the disaster-stricken town, though this idea is again quickly
warded off.

The acceptance of deprivations as a lesson expresses submission to the punishing authority. Any doubts which the
victim may have about the moral façade of the punisher are
repressed; the inflictions undergone are accepted as having
a noble and benevolent purpose. Such compliance may be
the outcome of conflicting feelings towards the punishing

agent, whether human or supernatural. There may at first be resentment and doubts as to the goodness of one who imposes such hardships. But from this there follows a terrifying sense of loss as the source of protection and love (whether human parent or divine father) seems to disappear, to become bad or non-existent. The need to reaffirm the existence of the good authority is thus intensified. The first impression in the moment of impact, as suggested by the images which I have cited (it was like someone hitting you over the head, etc.), is of a brutal attack. If this is punishment, it is at the hands of a wholly unloving punisher. But this painful impression is replaced on subsequent reflection by the image of a God who is very solicitous for the victims, and who has shown this by sparing them still worse inflictions. Out of the need for positive relations in the future to this authority, there is the resolve to lead a better life.

Following a disaster there may thus be an intensification of religious faith and observances and a heightening of moral standards. "Well, the whole family try to live better, I guess. We go to church oftener."[381] "It just makes you feel a little different—have a better outlook on life. In other words, don't regard it so lightly."[382] We have already noted the tendency towards increased asceticism in the resolve to care less about earthly treasures and more about heavenly ones. The need to stress the goodness of God, which, as I have suggested, may be partly a defense against resentment for inflictions suffered, also finds expression. And it is manifestly out of gratitude for this goodness, rather than in compliance with the punishment undergone, that disaster victims feel the urge to become more religious and virtuous. "Everybody seems to be thankful that it wasn't any worse and they all—some of them—seem to think that since they got through this that they will turn over a new leaf and try to live a better life."[383] Speaking of a Youth for Christ movement which had started among the high school students following the tornado, a citizen of San Angelo says: "Oh, they read the Bible and they have confession and witnessing for Christ. And you would be surprised some of these boys that would get up and witness for Christ. They knew Christ was with them during that time or they would not have been saved."[384]

The need to deny a terrible loss may also lead to the revival or intensification of religious faith. A woman whose little girl was killed in a catastrophe speaks of having been haunted by the image of her child's mangled body until she suddenly had a vision of the little girl happy in heaven. At the same time, though she had only been a perfunctory church-goer before, she experienced a sense of direct communication with God, the Father, who assured her that her little girl was safe with Him. Some people might react to such a disaster with a loss of faith: if such things can happen, God does not exist. For this woman, in her grief, the need to reaffirm the existence of a good and loving divine Father was just as great as, and inseparable from, her need to believe that her dead child was alive and happy.

The disaster in which this woman lost her child happened in Flagler, Colorado, at an air show, when a stunting plane crashed into the crowd. As the mother tells of her tragedy: "I looked around and there she was, laying on the ground. One of her arms was gone, the back of her head was gone. . . All I could see was Janie laying there. That's all I could see. But now that I know she's in Heaven, I can talk more calm about it. She's with God, the Father. . . There at first I guess I was in a terrible state of shock. I couldn't breathe. I thought —Bill said he just knew I was going to die, you know, before it was over. But something come to me then that Janie was happy wherever she was, after all this happened. I knew she was in Heaven. . . For the first thirty-six hours I just couldn't believe it, I just couldn't. All I could see was Janie laying there all dressed in bright red. To think she was so alive that morning, and then she was gone. . . And then something told me that I saw her in Heaven, and I have more of a calmness. If it hadn't been for that, I don't know how I'd ever have lived through it. . . I could see her. Something just came to me and took all that awful hurt and ache in my heart away. I knew she was in Heaven. That's the only place she could have been. She was such an angel here on earth. . . I had that awful aching, you know, in my heart, just feeling like I couldn't get my—couldn't breathe. That's all I could think of was Janie laying there like that. Then, this vision I had— she was in Heaven. That's all I could see. After that I knew she was happy, even though we were sad she was gone. . . You really have to have faith to live through anything like that. And before that, why my husband never did even believe in God. But after that, you know that we've erred from God. Why, I used to go to church once in a while, you know, just to be going, as a pattern of life. But when God revealed to me that my daughter was in Heaven, that she was safe and happy, why, that was really when first that awful ache was gone from me. You just have to have faith, or you couldn't hardly—I don't know how anybody could carry on."[385]

The belief that the dead live on is inseparable from the belief in a God who has the power to give this renewed life. Because of the need to deny death when it is immediate and unbearable, intensification of faith, or conversion, would seem more likely reactions than loss of faith under the impact of acute deprivation. I would suggest that loss of faith, if it occurs, is more apt to come later in a time of less severe stress, in response to some slighter stimulus which recalls (perhaps unconsciously) the earlier misfortune. Thus a young girl tells me that at the age of sixteen, when she was reading *Crime and Punishment,* she became very depressed and suddenly realized that there was no God and no immortality. Her mother had died five years before. At that time the girl had continued to believe in God and thought of her mother as being in heaven. It would have been too painful for her to think that her mother was wholly dead. The story of the murder of the old woman in *Crime and Punishment* apparently aroused feelings associated with her mother's death, which, though depressing, were no longer overwhelming, so that doubts about the existence of a good God could break through and the belief in immortality could be abandoned.

Those who survive a disaster in which others perish may naturally be inclined to feel that this is due to some superiority in themselves. An elderly woman tells how the day after the bombing of Nagasaki she encountered a young woman among the ruins, blithely washing clothes at the well, who greeted her with: "Well, Grandma Moriuchi, God must love both of us, mustn't he? I'd never thought I was such an especially good person but I guess I must be, after all, for it was only God's special grace that I wasn't killed. I'm so happy that God wanted to spare me! Those people who were burned to death, they must have made God angry, mustn't they? They must have provoked him to wrath. You must be a good person too, Grandma. You've just been hurt a little."[386] (This complacent attitude is, incidentally, cited with great disapproval. As we shall see in a moment, the little group from Nagasaki who wrote their memoirs suffered not only from their losses but also from intense self-reproaches.)

Such a tendency towards self-congratulation is often countered by dread that one will be penalized for being too confident of one's luck. The ancient Greeks spoke of *hubris*, a mortal's overestimation of himself, which must inevitably draw down the anger of the gods. Thus Ajax, inordinately proud of his strength in arms, boasted that he would win the war of Troy without the help of the gods, and they drove him to madness, ignominy, and suicide.[387] The man who does not recognize that any good fortune is for the gods to give or take away as they see fit will thus provoke a devastating demonstration of the might of the superior powers. For Christians there is the sin of pride. This would be exemplified if one reveled in one's good fortune or presumed it to be one's due. Thus among the survivors of a tornado in Arkansas: "It seems like when you go to church on Sunday morning the people are more humble."[388]

The survivor who defends himself against the temptation of supposing he deserved his good fortune because of already acquired merit may decide that he must do something in the future to be worthy of it. A woman from Arkansas says: "Why we were left here, I don't know. I think we should search ourselves and find out whether ... maybe we were left here to help someone else.... And I hope to put myself to good use from here on out, the rest of my life, to prove to people that I want to be worthy of being spared."[389] And according to another: "I really feel that we were all spared for some purpose. I feel that these last two weeks maybe that I was supposed to go down and help these people (at the relief agency where she had worked)... There will be something come up in my life yet in a short while that I really will know that I was left here for some purpose... When you look around here and see all the other homes and things that have been destroyed and you are left, it really makes you think a little bit."[390] For these people having survived is not taken as a reward for virtue, something one can accept as one's due. That would be too proud an attitude and would imply a condescending judgment on those who lost their lives. Rather in having been spared one has incurred a debt to the power that saved one, and this must be repaid by future good deeds. We see in this defense against pride another motive for asceticism and intensified moral striving following a disaster.

Survivors may also feel that there is really no difference in merit between them and those who succumbed. Their resolve to lead a better life may then be not a defense against pride but rather an effort to ward off a chastisement which they feel they have escaped only by some oversight. It is as if the powers, like hasty parents, had struck some of their children and not others when all were equally blameworthy. But perhaps on the morrow there may be a more careful reckoning and it will be the turn of those to be punished who escaped without deserving it. The urge of the survivor to acquire further merit may be motivated on these grounds. If he can show how anxious he is to be good, the powers may decide that he deserves his exemption from punishment.

But there are also circumstances in which there is an opposite reaction to having survived extreme hazards. Instead of feeling impelled towards greater virtue, the survivor may experience a relaxation of moral demands. The disaster may have the significance of a *memento mori,* stimulating a vivid awareness of how little time there is to enjoy all the pleasures which one has been putting off. This is apt to be the more so where there is reason to anticipate an imminent return of the danger. Thus in the region around Nagasaki it is reported that after the bomb fell: "There were many farmers who ate their cows and chickens. They said, 'Let's have a good time while we're here on earth, we won't be much longer—the atom bomb means it's all up with the world.' "[391] In such a situation the individual's time perspective is radically altered. The long-term aims for the sake of which he has denied himself immediate indulgence become so uncertain that the sacrifice of present pleasure seems pointless.

There are other situations where surviving a hazard brings an elated sense of immunity and liberation from restraints. Here it is not a question of making haste to enjoy life for tomorrow we die. Rather there is the feeling that since one has survived the ordeal one is utterly absolved; there is no punishment, no death, and everything is permitted. Thus there is the orgiastic reaction of soldiers who have passed unscathed through the ordeal of battle, the sense of liberation from moral anxiety and intensified pleasure in life of patients who have survived an operation,[392] the sometimes unruly demonstrations of students who have just finished a severe and crucial examination like that of the *bachot* in Paris. The sense of release which may occur in such instances may arise from a feeling that having undergone the ordeal constitutes payment in full for all the enjoyment which the individual now feels he can permit himself. But perhaps in anticipating the ordeal, the student, the patient, the soldier have doubted whether they could survive. They have felt that a terrible day of reckoning was at hand. The fact that they have come through it has disproved their fears, and seems to show that the ordeal was not intended as a punishment for their sins. With this there is a relaxation of moral tension, a feeling of being at one with one's conscience. The survivor of the ordeal experiences elation.

Such ordeals differ from undergoing a sudden disaster. The ordeal is anticipated and various preparations are made which may include precautionary self-denial. In surviving an ordeal, the individual feels that he has passed a test of his strength or skill, where the survivor of a disaster more often feels that he has come through only by luck or grace. Thus the sense of orgiastic liberation after surviving a fearful danger would seem more apt to occur in the kind of ordeal which I have indicated rather than following a sudden disaster.

Yet another reaction to disaster is defiance of the powers that be. For all the losses he has suffered the individual takes the obstinate stance of the child who, however severely punished, keeps his jaws clenched and does not emit a cry or a tear. He demonstrates to the punishing authorities: you can't hurt me! Thus in a Mexican town, devastated by a flood, "Lower class people would remark, 'The flood didn't hurt us—we never had anything anyway.' Businessmen would say, 'When we make a profit it is taken in taxes, so what is the difference.' "[393] There is an effort to make oneself invulnerable in such an attitude of expecting no good and fearing no evil. This defiance of fate and proclaiming that one is unimpressed by its furious onslaught is in marked contrast to the grateful and humble feelings which we have observed in other survivors of disaster.

I should now like to add something further on the problem of assigning blame for a disaster. I have spoken of natural catastrophes and the alternatives of the victims blaming their gods or blaming themselves or struggling to find some interpretation that is mutually exonerating. Where a disaster is man-made further possibilities and conflicts about the assignment of blame enter in. In the war-time bombing of civilian populations, the enemy is the obvious target for rage and indignation. But also blame may be directed against the authorities on one's own side for not providing sufficient protection.[394] The impact of a disaster stimulates feelings of helplessness and intensified longings to be taken care of. Where the agencies that are looked to for the satisfaction of such needs are felt to be disappointing there is apt to be anger and resentment towards them. One of the survivors of Hiroshima who was struggling ineffectually to help the wounded and dying experienced such a reaction as he thought of the sources of medical aid which should have been there but failed to come. He "suddenly thought of the naval hospital ship, which had not come (it never did), and he had for a moment a feeling of blind, murderous rage at the crew of the ship, and then at all doctors. Why didn't they come to help these people?"[395] In a similar way, we have seen how following a disaster resentment often arises against relief agencies because of the disappointments which people suffer in not getting the compensation for which they had hoped. In such instances we might say that resentment and reproaches are directed less against the bad parent figures who have inflicted the pain and damage than against the good parent figures who are expected to make it all good again.

In catastrophic accidents other questions about who is to blame present themselves. A major alternative here is that between blaming the immediate precipitating cause and assigning responsibility to more general conditioning factors. In the case of the Cocoanut Grove fire,[396] the question was first raised: who started it? The newspapers discovered that it was a busboy who lit a match to replace a missing light bulb who had set off the fatal blaze. This exposure was met by a strong public reaction that this boy should not be blamed. The boy, a high school student, received numerous fan letters, some enclosing money, and there were proposals that he receive an appointment to West Point. We might think it manifestly irrational to blame a person who had unwittingly precipitated such a catastrophe. But there is probably a deep-lying inclination to blame the one who, however unintentionally and by however small an act, sets off a disaster. "Woe to him through whom evil cometh!" This initial reaction, however, arouses conflicting feelings, especially where the precipitating agent is otherwise an object of sympathy. One cannot with a clear conscience cast such a burden of guilt on the shoulders of a nice young boy. The popular enthusiasm for this youth may have been in part a reaction formation against an initial impulse to blame him. Other and less immediate objects of blame were then sought whose appropriateness, while in part quite realistic, was also determined by their being already objects of resentment. These were city officials, who were accused of not setting up or enforcing adequate standards of public safety, and the owners of the nightclub, the exploitative rich who build places of expensive amusement out of cheap and flimsy materials. Actually there was only one owner, but the generalization expressed in the term "the owners" facilitated the release and intensification of resentments already present in relation to a class frequently regarded with envy and dislike. Thus an object of blame was found, indignation against whom had massive antecedent moral sanctions. Neither the newspapers nor the public, in their letters to the press, blamed the panic of the victims which had led to the fatal crush and to the blocking of the exits. It is exceedingly difficult to blame those who perish in a catastrophe.

In the disaster at the race track of Le Mans, where a car crashed into a retaining wall and exploded, and its engine and other parts, hurled into the crowd, killed seventy-seven people, the problem of assignment of blame was extremely complicated.[397] The drivers involved in the accident, the mechanical features of the fatal car, the different national groups represented in the race, the construction of the track, the organizers of the race, the rules governing racing, the rationale of racing in general, the nature of progress, the relation of man to the tools and playthings he creates, and fate were severally and in combination called to account. I shall not here attempt to sort out all the arguments which ensued. Rather I shall confine myself to some aspects of the issue between immediate precipitating causes and more remote and general factors.

The fatal car, of German make, a Mercedes, was driven by a Frenchman, Levegh. An English driver in a Jaguar (who eventually won the race) had cut in abruptly to go to his refueling stand, forcing the car behind him, an Austin, to veer to the left, and it was in trying to avoid this latter car that Levegh crashed. It is difficult, as I have said, to blame a person who himself loses his life in the catastrophe. In the newspapers, Levegh, so far from being an agent of destruc-

tion, appeared as a saviour. It was said that his last gesture
was a warning signal to Fangio, another Mercedes driver,
coming up immediately behind him. Fangio was widely
quoted as saying: "Levegh saved my life." One newspaper
carried this saviour theme still further in saying that at the
last moment Levegh had turned his wheel to prevent his car
from going over into the crowd, and so had saved the lives
of many other people who otherwise would have been killed.
However, the impulse to blame him through whom evil
cometh was not entirely repressed. According to an account
current in some Paris bistros Levegh was indeed the mur-
derer of all the innocent victims in the crowd. The argument went like this: Levegh had the choice of saving his
fellow driver or veering towards the crowd. He chose the
latter alternative because of his greater loyalty to one of his
own. Behind this reasoning there was the conviction of common people that the elite stick together against them.

The question of the culpability of the Jaguar driver
resolves itself into the alternatives: either he made a small
error in cutting to the side a bit too abruptly, from which
no grave consequences could have been anticipated, or he
willingly risked the destruction of scores of people to gain
a few seconds in his mad desire to win. Since the ascription
of such grandiose villainy to a blond young English sports-
man seemed incongruous, the preferred view was that he
made at most a small mistake. Other drivers in giving evidence in the investigation were inclined to say that no one
driver could be blamed; it was rather a question of the very
high speed of contemporary race course driving, which made
perfect control impossible.

A diversion of attention from the causes of the catastrophe
was provided by the circumstance that the race was not
stopped. Though the accident had occurred near the beginning of the scheduled twenty-four hours, the race was allowed
to continue to the end. There were many recriminations
about this unfeeling behavior which were countered by jus-
tifications and counter-recriminations. The French papers
naturally took offense at the indignation expressed abroad.

The Germans had assumed a particularly moralizing tone, strengthened by the fact that the German firm, Mercedes, had withdrawn its contestants following the accident. The French press retorted that the Germans were hardly in a position to pass judgment on others—had they forgotten their recent record of atrocities? What I would like to bring out about this controversy is that it served to displace a good deal of strong feeling from the question of the cause of death to that of proper decorum towards the dead. So, similarly, after a funeral there may be family disputes about who failed to come and who did not wear proper mourning. Even in cases of natural death, on the unconscious level there persists the belief that it was murder. In the effort to ward off this more serious accusation, the survivors may displace their attention to the question of who did not show proper respect to the dead.

The catastrophe evoked many reflections in the press on the nature of man and the nature of progress. Man was likened to the sorcerer's apprentice, who unleashed forces which he then could not control, or to Icarus, who in his overbold attempt at flight plunged headlong into the sea. There were headshakings over progress, which demands so many human sacrifices. The deaths of the victims at Le Mans were thus invested with a significance of metaphysical tragedy. Looking at the disaster in this lofty way served to avoid assigning blame to anyone. A similar function was served later by the reports on the investigations of experts in which it was said to be nearly impossible to determine exactly what had happened. Thus scientific uncertainties about details and distant metaphysical views may operate equally as defenses against blame.

Another aspect of blame in connection with disasters is the tendency of survivors to blame themselves for not having done enough for those who perished. We have seen before that survival may be taken as a mark of goodness, an occasion for intensified self-esteem. Sometimes, however, the opposite reaction appears: the survivor feels guilty for not having died instead of his loved ones, or in an effort to save them.

Such self-reproach forms a leitmotiv in the memoirs of a little group of survivors of Nagasaki.[398] A woman whose mother was killed torments herself with the thought, "Surely she called my name with her last breath. And where was I? Hiding in the shelter at Topposui." When later her brother returns from the army, she confesses to him that their mother is dead, and as they weep together, "the sound seemed to accuse me, it seemed to be saying, 'You killed your mother!'" Dr. Nagai, who collected these stories, says of this remorseful daughter: "Right before her eyes had been the burning town with her mother somewhere inside, but she made no attempt to dash through the fire to save her. To this day it torments Tatsue to remember her lack of courage. Unquestionably, even if she had dared the flames, it would have been too late to save her mother; yet whenever she hears the story of how Mrs. Tsuchie from next door had rushed into the fire, trying to save her child and getting badly burned in the attempt, inside her she feels deeply ashamed."

Such guilt is not mitigated by the realization that one could not have saved those who perished or by any extenuating circumstances. Thus in another case, that of a young boy, Dr. Nagai says, "Did he not stay down in the air-raid shelter and forget all about his mother and sister and brothers? To this day the memory pricks his conscience. Of course, he was just a grade school boy and he had sustained an injury to his head, so surely it was perfectly natural that it should not occur to him to try and save them. Nonetheless, Satoru has lost faith in himself." Dr. Nagai adds his own self-reproaches, that instead of running home to his wife (who, as it later turned out, was already dead) he stayed at his post in the hospital because he wanted to be considered a hero. Then, finding a still more discreditable motive, he says that he did not go home, and thus left wounded neighbors to die uncared for, because he was afraid another bomb would fall on the city. And he sums it up: "Those who survived the atom bomb were people who ignored their friends crying out *in extremis;* or who shook off wounded neighbors who clung to them, pleading to be saved... Those who survived the bomb were, if not merely lucky, in a greater or lesser degree selfish, self-centered, guided by instinct more than by civilization . . . and we know it, we who have survived. Knowing it is a dull ache without surcease."

The susceptibility to such self-reproach is individually and also culturally variable. The guilt of these survivors of Nagasaki would seem to be related to the traditional Japanese acceptance of an oppressive burden of family obligations.[399] Underlying these heavy familial duties we may suspect intensely ambivalent feelings towards family members, feelings which incessant performance of duty aims to control, and which occasion strong self-reproaches in case of any lapse. In this conception of duty, correct performance is required regardless of utility or hindering circumstance. So, for example, a daughter should run through fire to save her mother. That her mother, as it turns out, was past saving does not exonerate her. Her failure in her duty is felt as a break-through of her negative feelings towards her mother and leads to the self-accusation: I killed her. In the case of Dr. Nagai and his relatives, their conversion to Christianity seems to have had the effect of adding to familial obligations an equally inexorable duty to one's neighbor. Thus Dr. Nagai adds deficiency in love for their neighbors to his reckoning of the guilt of the survivors. "The fact that they survived when friends and loved ones died; that when faced by the grim choice, they left those to perish that their own skins might be saved; that they loved not their neighbor—will press down upon their souls."

There is thus a range of possibilities for the direction of blame, against oneself or against others, with the choice in the latter case among specific and general causes, mechanical, human and supernatural. There may be, as we have seen, conflicting feelings about assigning blame to one or another agency, and various devices for deflecting it. Again, what is selected as the blameworthy aspect of a disastrous situation varies. Also there are differences, between individuals and between groups, in the strength of the need to assign blame or the capacity to feel that no one is to blame: it's just one of those things. These alternative reactions would seem to be related to latent hostilities and antecedent attitudes about responsibility. Probably the more latent hostility there is present in an individual the greater will be his need to blame either himself or others for destructive happenings. Where, on the other hand, such latent hostility is slight, there would be less of a tendency to attribute the damage to bad intentions. As to the many possible beliefs about responsibility, let me mention only the degree to which people feel responsible for others or consider each man responsible for himself, and the extent to which responsibility may be qualified by considerations of what is feasible.

We have observed the tendency towards avoidance of blame, exoneration of God and man, in American disaster victims. A study of reactions to disaster based on American material found that even in the case of man-made catastrophes there were few expressions of resentment.[400] There also seems to be little of the self-reproach on the part of survivors of the sort which we have heard expressed by some Japanese. So, for instance, in an episode in Atlanta, Georgia, where many died from drinking poison whiskey, a man says laughingly, about a friend and drinking companion who succumbed: "He must have drunk more. No, he just didn't know how to take it."[401] Thus he jokingly assimilates fatality to getting dead drunk; his friend didn't know how to hold his liquor. The assumption behind such a reaction would seem to be that everyone is responsible for taking his own risks, and that a man shouldn't get into something he can't handle.

Where one does feel responsible for others, there is an effort to qualify duty in terms of feasibility, not to blame oneself for not doing what is beyond one's powers. A woman from Worcester whose mother was killed and whose husband was injured in the tornado expresses this.[402] She left her mother's body lying on the ground in order to accompany her husband to the hospital. A day or two later she left her husband in the hospital to attend her mother's funeral in another town. She evidently felt some compunction about both these things, but also tried to reassure herself that she was justified in what she did. Speaking of her mother, she says, "I think about how I saw her. I can't forget that. Because I did see her when I went by with my husband on the stretcher and I knew I couldn't help her so there was no point in stopping." Thus she opposes her feelings of guilt for not staying beside her mother's body with the reflection that there was nothing she could have done for her mother, there was "no point." This may not eliminate the guilt, but at least there is the feeling: one need not blame oneself for such things. Similarly about leaving her husband in order to arrange her mother's funeral, she says: "I knew my husband was in good hands and was being well cared for." Though she feels some qualms about having left him, she reassures herself that she was not indispensably needed. We may suppose that this woman's self-reproaches were reduced by the fact that in each instance (of leaving her mother, and leaving her husband) she was performing an urgent duty. However, where the impulse to blame oneself is greater, and one's sense of responsibility is less qualified by realistic limitations, this may not be exonerating. We may recall that in the case of Dr. Nagai, his staying at the hospital to care for many injured persons did not, to his way of feeling, absolve him for his failure to run home to his wife.

We have seen in what a variety of different ways people react to disasters. But there are also certain feelings about catastrophes which are very widespread, which we find recurring in many times and places. Of these the one which I have found to be the most recurrent is the view of disaster as the great equalizer. The high are made low. Earthly injustices are rectified. In the face of overwhelming danger and imminent death all men are equal. In the vision of the final cataclysm in the Book of Revelation, we read: "And lo, there was a great earthquake; and the sun became black as sackcloth of hair, and the moon became as blood. And the stars of heaven fell into the earth . . . and every mountain and island were moved out of their places. And the kings of the earth, and the great men, and the rich men, and the chief captains, and the mighty men, and every bondman, and every free man, hid themselves in the dens and in the rocks of the mountains."

Ignazio Silone, speaking about the earthquake in his native Abruzzi in 1915, reflects: an earthquake buries rich and poor, learned and illiterate, rulers and subjects beneath its ruins. It achieves what the law promises and fails to fulfill, the equality of all men. It is for this reason, according to Silone, that the Italians show such endurance and equanimity in the face of natural catastrophes.[403]

In the ruins of Nagasaki, a woman came upon a cousin of hers, severely wounded, who begged her to help him to a priest so that he might take the sacrament (they were Christians). As she assists the suffering and fainting man, despite her pity for him, she cannot resist thinking how here a formerly proud person has been humbled. "In the past he had often swaggered around acting important. But now that he knew death's visit was near he had become very humble, earnestly clinging to the hand of God as he climbed the sloping road to the church."[404]

After a tornado in Arkansas, a woman has this to say: "We got a lot of people get so high up in the world, think they own it and everything that's in it and everything else. And it takes something like this to bring them down equal."[405]

Notes

Abbreviations for sources most frequently cited:

Janis—Janis, Irving, *Air War and Emotional Stress: Psychological Studies of Bombing and Civilian Defense*, McGraw-Hill, New York, 1951.

NORC—Marks, Eli S., Charles E. Fritz, and others, *Human Reactions in Disaster Situations*, Report No. 52, National Opinion Research Center, 3 vols. June 1954. (Being reproduced by the Armed Services Technical Information Agency).

Powell—Powell, John Walker, *An Introduction to the Natural History of Disaster*, Unpublished Report, Baltimore: Psychiatric Institute of the University of Maryland, June 1954 (mimeographed).

Schmideberg—Schmideberg, Melitta, Some Observations on Individual Reactions to Air Raids, *International Journal of Psychoanalysis, 23,* 1942, pp. 146-75.

U. of Md.—Protocols of interviews with disaster victims, collected by the Disaster Research Project, Psychiatric Institute of the University of Maryland (mimeographed).

U. of Texas—Protocols of interviews with disaster victims, collected by the Waco-San Angelo Disaster Study, Department of Sociology, University of Texas (typed ms.).

Wallace—Wallace, Anthony F. C., *Tornado in Worcester: An Exploratory Study of Individual and Community Behavior in an Extreme Situation*, Committee on Disaster Studies, Disaster Study No. 3, National Academy of Sciences—National Research Council, Publication No. 392, Washington, D. C., 1956.

1. Angus Campbell, Sylvia Eberhart, and Patricia Woodward, *Public Reaction to the Atomic Bomb and World Affairs, A Nation-wide Survey of Attitudes and Information*, Cornell University, Ithaca, New York, 1947.

2. Ernst Kris & Nathan Leites, Trends in 20th Century Propaganda, in *Reader in Public Opinion and Communication*, Bernard Berelson & Morris Janowitz, eds., The Free Press, Glencoe, Illinois, 1950.

3. Campbell, Eberhart and Woodward, *op. cit.*

4. Janis.

5. Mildred Borgum, The Fear of Explosion, *American Journal of Orthopsychiatry, 14*, 1944, pp. 349-58; cf. E. Stengel, Air Raid Phobia, *British Journal of Medical Psychology, 20*, 1944, pp. 135-43.

6. Ernest Jones, Psychology and War Conditions, *Papers on Psychoanalysis*, 5th edition, Baillière, Tindall, & Cox, London, 1948, pp. 173-95.

7. Schmideberg.

8. *Ibid.*

9. I. Atkin, Air Raid Strain in Mental Hospital Admissions, *Lancet, 241*, 1941, pp. 72-4.

10. Stengel, *op. cit.*

11. Ernest Jones, War Shock and Freud's Theory of the Neuroses, *Papers on Psychoanlysis*, 3rd edition, Baillière, Tindall, & Cox, London, 1923, pp. 577-94.

12. Richard M. Titmuss, *Problems of Social Policy*, His Majesty's Stationery Office, London, 1950.

13. Schmideberg.

14. Janis; NORC; Enrico L. Quarantelli, *A Study of Panic: Its Nature, Types, and Conditions*, University of Chicago, July 1953 (unpublished Master's thesis).

15. Janis.

16. Otto Fenichel, *The Psychoanalytic Theory of Neurosis*, Norton, New York, 1945.

17. Geoffrey Gorer, *Exploring English Character*, Cresset Press, London, 1955.

18. Otto Fenichel, The Counter-Phobic Attitude, *Collected Papers*, 2nd series, Norton, New York, 1954, pp. 163-73.

20. David P. Boder, personal communication; cf. his *I Did Not Interview the Dead*, University of Illinois Press, Urbana, Illinois, 1949.

21. Bruno Bettelheim, Individual and Mass Behavior in Extreme Situations, *Journal of Abnormal and Social Psychology, 38*, 1943, pp. 417-52.

22. Leonard Logan, Lewis M. Killian, & Wyatt Marrs, *A Study of the Effect of Catastrophe on Social Disorganization*, Technical Memorandum ORO-T-194, Johns Hopkins University, Operations Research Office, Chevy Chase, Maryland, July 1952.

23. U. of Texas.

24. University of Oklahoma Research Institute, *The Kansas City Flood and Fire of 1951*, Technical Memorandum ORO-T-203, Johns Hopkins University, Operations Research Office, Chevy Chase, Maryland, August 1952.

25. *Ibid.*

26. *Ibid.*

27. *Ibid.*

28. *Ibid.*

29. Schmideberg.

30. U. of Texas.

31. Nathan Leites, personal communication.

32. Powell.

33. Mark Zborowski & Elizabeth Herzog, *Life is with People*, International Universities Press, New York, 1952; Martha Wolfenstein, Two Types of Jewish Mothers, in *Childhood in Contemporary Cultures*, Margaret Mead & Martha Wolfenstein, eds., University of Chicago Press, Chicago, Illinois, 1955, pp. 424-42.

34. Nathan Leites, *A Study of Bol-*

shevism, The Free Press, Glencoe, Illinois, 1953.

35. Margaret Mead, *And Keep Your Powder Dry*, Morrow, New York, 1943.

36. NORC.

37. U. of Texas.

38. *Ibid.*

39. U. of Oklahoma Research Institute, *op. cit.*

40. *Ibid.*

41. *Ibid.*

42. NORC.

43. *Ibid.*

44. U. of Texas.

45. R. R. Grinker & B. W. Willerman, A Study of Psychological Predisposition to the Development of Operational Fatigue, *American Journal of Orthopsychiatry, 16,* 1946, pp. 191-214.

46. Janis.

47. H. Wilson, Mental Reactions to Air Raids, *Lancet, 242,* 1942, pp. 284-87; Adolph G. Woltman, Life on a Target, *American Journal of Orthopsychiatry, 15,* 1945, pp. 172-77.

48. Ernst Kris, Danger and Morale, *American Journal of Orthopsychiatry, 14,* 1944, pp. 147-55.

49. Janis.

50. U. of Md.

51. Schmideberg.

52. U. of Texas.

53. Schmideberg.

54. Janis.

55. Marie Bonaparte, *Myths of War*, Imago, London, 1947.

56. Schmideberg.

57. Irving Janis, *Psychological Stress* (in preparation).

58. Joost A. M. Meerloo, *Patterns of Panic*, International Universities Press, New York, 1950.

59. C. Diggory & A. Pepitone, *Behavior and Disaster*, University of Pennsylvania, 1953 (mimeographed).

60. *Ibid.*

61. U. of Texas.

62. Schmideberg.

63. U. of Texas.

64. *Ibid.*

65. *Ibid.*

66. *Ibid.*

67. Schmideberg.

68. U. of Texas.

69. Area Research Center, Michigan State College, Operation Rio Grande, Preliminary Progress Report, September, 1954 (mimeographed).

70. Elias Colbert & Everett Chamberlin, *Chicago and the Great Conflagration*, Vent, New York, 1871.

71. University of Oklahoma Research Institute, *op. cit.*

72. Janis; Schmideberg.

73. NORC.

74. Janis.

75. NORC.

76. Leonard Logan, *Report on England's 1953 Flood Disaster*, Committee on Disaster Studies, National Academy of Sciences—National Research Council, 1953, Unpublished Report (typed ms.).

77. J. B. Green and Leonard Logan, *The South Amboy Disaster*, A Special Report, Johns Hopkins University, Operations Research Office, Chevy Chase, Maryland, August 1950.

78. J. B. Ellemers & Henny M. in' Veld-Langeveld, The Study of the Destruction of a Community, in *Studies in Holland Flood Disaster 1953*, Vol. III, The Institute for Social Research in the Netherlands, Amsterdam, and the National Academy of Sciences—National Research Council, Washington, D. C., 1955, pp. 75-114.

79. Father Siemes, S. J., Hiroshima, August 6, 1945, *Bulletin of the Atomic Scientists, 1,* May 15, 1946, pp. 2-6.

80. Takashi Nagai, *We of Nagasaki*, Duell, Sloan & Pearce, New York, 1951.

81. Wallace.

82. NORC.

83. Wallace.

84. NORC.
85. U. of Md.
86. NORC.
87. Janis.
88. Ignazio Silone in *The God That Failed*, Richard Crossman, ed., Harper, New York, 1950.
89. Logan, Killian, & Marrs, *op. cit.;* NORC.
90. Schmideberg.
91. Unpublished interviews by Charlotte Roland on the disaster of Le Mans, June 1955.
92. Logan, Killian, & Marrs, *op. cit.;* NORC.
93. Sigmund Freud, *The Problem of Anxiety*, Norton, New York, 1936.
94. Janis.
95. U. of Texas.
96. NORC.
97. U. of Texas.
98. NORC.
99. Powell.
100. U. of Md.
101. NORC.
102. *Ibid.*
103. U. of Md.
104. Logan, Killian, & Marrs, *op. cit.*
105. NORC.
106. Sigmund Freud, A Religious Experience, *Collected Papers*, Vol. 5, Hogarth Press, London, 1950, pp. 243-46.
107. NORC, *Conference on Field Studies of Reactions to Disaster*, University of Chicago, Report No. 47, January 1953.
108. Bettelheim, *op. cit.*
109. Anna Freud, *The Ego and the Mechanisms of Defense*, International Universities Press, New York, 1946; Anna Freud & Dorothy Burlingham, *Young Children in Wartime*, Allen & Unwin, London, 1942; J. Louise Despert, *Preliminary Report on Children's Reactions to the War*, Cornell University, 1942; Janis; Stewart Perry, Earle Silber, & Donald A. Bloch, *Children in Disaster*, Committee on Disaster Studies, National Academy of Sciences—National Research Council, Washington, 1955 (mimeographed).
110. Robert Waelder, Psychoanalytic Aspects of War and Peace, *Geneva Studies*, volume 10, number 2, Geneva Research Center, May 1939, pp. 1-56.
111. Janis.
112. Schmideberg.
113. NORC.
114. Perry, Silber, & Bloch, *op cit.;* U. of Texas; Wallace.
115. Janis; J. T. MacCurdy, *The Structure of Morale*, Macmillan, New York, 1943.
116. Grinker & Willerman, *op cit.*
117. Alexander Adler, Neuropsychiatric Complications in Victims of Boston's Cocoanut Grove Disaster, *Journal of the American Medical Association, 123,* 1943, pp. 1098-1101.
118. Ernst Kris, *op. cit.*
119. Janis.
120. *Ibid.*
121. Wallace.
122. *Ibid.*
123. NORC.
124. U. of Md.
125. *Ibid.*
126. Wallace.
127. *Ibid.*
128. Alexander N. Hood, Personal Experiences in the Great Earthquake, *Living Age, 261,* May, 1909, pp. 355-65.
129. John Hersey, *Hiroshima*, Alfred Knopf, New York, 1954.
130. Logan, Killian, & Marrs, *op. cit.*
131. NORC.
132. U. of Texas.
133. U. of Md.
134. J. S. Tyhurst, Individual Reactions to Community Disaster, *American Journal of Psychiatry, 107,* 1951, pp. 764-69.
135. NORC.
136. Leonard Logan & Lewis M. Killian, *Troop Reactions to Atomic Attack: A Preview*, Technical Mem-

orandum ORO-T-205, Johns Hopkins University, Operations Research Office, Chevy Chase, Maryland, July 1952.

137. Fenichel, *The Psychoanalytic Theory of Neurosis;* Edward Bibring, The Mechanism of Depression, in *Affective Disorders,* Phyllis Greenacre, ed., International Universities Press, New York, 1953, pp. 13-48.

138. Fenichel, *op. cit.*

139. Schmideberg.

140. Otto E. Sperling, The Interpretation of the Trauma as a Command, *Psychoanalytic Quarterly, 19,* 1950, pp. 352-70.

141. Wallace; Powell.

142. Wallace.

143. Logan, Killian, & Marrs, *op. cit.*

144. Schmideberg.

145. *The Problem of Panic,* A Statement of the Committee on Disaster Studies, National Academy of Sciences—National Research Council, Technical Bulletin TB-19-2, Federal Civil Defense Administration, U. S. Government Printing Office, Washington, D. C., June 1955.

146. *Ibid.;* Janis; Quarantelli, *op. cit.;* Anselm Strauss, The Literature on Panic, *Journal of Abnormal and Social Psychology, 39,* 1944, pp. 317-28; John Rickman, Panic and Air-Raid Precautions, *Lancet, 234,* June 1938, pp. 1291-5.

147. Quarantelli, *op. cit.*

148. Hersey, *op. cit.*

149. *The Problem of Panic;* Quarantelli, *op. cit.;* Janis; Logan & Killian, *op. cit.;* Diggory & Pepitone, *op. cit.*

150. Schmideberg.

151. Robert Graves, *The Greek Myths,* Penguin, Harmondsworth, Middlesex, 1955.

152. Wallace.

153. U. of Md.

154. *Ibid.*

155. *Ibid.*

156. *Ibid.*

157. U. of Texas.

158. NORC.

159. *Ibid.*

160. *Ibid.*

161. NORC.

162. Zborowski & Herzog, *op. cit.;* Wolfenstein, *op. cit.*

163. NORC; Logan, Killian & Marrs, *op. cit.*

164. U. of Md.

165. *Ibid.*

166. U. of Texas.

167. U. of Md.

168. Hanson Baldwin, *Admiral Death,* Simon & Schuster, New York, 1939.

169. *Ibid.*

170. Schmideberg; Janis.

171. Colbert and Chamberlin, *op. cit.*

172. *Ibid.*

173. Schmideberg; Janis.

174. Freud, *The Problem of Anxiety, op. cit.*

175. Mark Zborowski, Cultural Components in Responses to Pain, *Journal of Social Issues, 8,* 1952, pp. 16-30.

176. NORC.

177. Hood, *op. cit.*

178. Children's Bureau, Department of Labor, *Infant Care,* Government Printing Office, Washington, D. C., 1951; Martha Wolfenstein, Fun Morality: An Analysis of Recent American Child-training Literature, in *Childhood in Contemporary Cultures,* Margaret Mead & Martha Wolfenstein, eds., University of Chicago Press, Chicago, Illinois, 1955, pp. 168-78.

179. Powell.

180. Logan, Killian & Marrs, *op. cit.*

181. U. of Md.

182. U. of Texas.

183. *Ibid.*

184. *Ibid.*

185. *Ibid.*

186. *Ibid.*

187. *Ibid.*

188. *Ibid.*

189. Margaret Mead, *And Keep Your Powder Dry, op. cit.*

190. U. of Texas.

191. *Ibid.*

192. *Ibid.*

193. U. of Md.

194. NORC.

195. U. of Texas.

196. U. of Md.

197. *Ibid.*

198. Wallace.

199. U. of Md.

201. NORC.

202. U. of Md.

203. Logan, Killian & Marrs, *op. cit.*

204. U. of Texas.

205. *Ibid.*

206. NORC.

207. U. of Texas.

208. U. of Md.

209. Hersey, *op. cit.*

210. William James, On Some Mental Effects of the Earthquake, *Memories and Studies*, Longmans Green, New York, 1911.

211. Ellemers & Veld-Langeveld, *op. cit.*

212. Sigmund Freud, Humour, *Collected Papers*, volume 5, Hogarth, London, 1950, pp. 215-21.

213. U. of Texas.

214. NORC.

215. *Ibid.*

216. *Ibid.*

217. U. of Texas.

218. U. of Md.

219. Logan, Killian & Marrs, *op. cit.*

220. U. of Texas.

221. NORC.

222. *Ibid.*

223. U. of Texas.

224. NORC.

225. Fenichel, *op. cit.*

226. *Ibid.*

227. U. of Texas.

228. *Ibid.*

229. NORC.

230. U. of Texas.

231. Perry, Silber & Bloch, *op. cit.*

232. Sigmund Freud, Mourning and Melancholia, *Collected Papers*, volume 4, Hogarth Press, London, 1946, pp. 152-72.

233. Sigmund Freud, From the History of an Infantile Neurosis, *Collected Papers*, volume 3, Hogarth Press, 1946, pp. 473-605.

234. Erich Lindemann, The Symptomatology and Management of Acute Grief, *American Journal of Psychiatry, 101*, 1944, pp. 141-48; Stanley Cobb & Erich Lindemann, Neuropsychiatric Observations following the Cocoanut Grove Disaster, *Annals of Surgery, 117*, 1943, pp. 814-24.

235. Roy R. Grinker & John P. Spiegel, *War Neuroses*, Blakiston, Philadelphia, 1945.

236. NORC.

237. U. of Texas.

238. Fenichel, *op. cit.*

239. Janis; Powell; NORC.

240. U. of Md.

241. U. of Texas.

242. *Ibid.*

243. Logan, Killian & Marrs, *op. cit.*

244. *Ibid.*

245. *Ibid.*

246. Logan, *Report on England's 1953 Flood Disaster, op. cit.*

247. Franz Alexander, in a discussion on Disaster Research at the Center for Advanced Study in the Behavioral Sciences, Palo Alto, January 26, 1955.

248. Schmideberg; Douglas D. Bond, *The Love and Fear of Flying*, International Universities Press, New York, 1952.

249. Fenichel, *op. cit.*

250. U. of Md.

251. U. of Texas.

252. *Ibid.*

253. *Ibid.*

254. NORC.

255. Omitted.

256. U. of Md.

257. NORC.
258. Perry, Silber & Bloch, *op. cit.*
259. U. of Texas.
260. *Ibid.*
261. *Ibid.*
262. *Ibid.*
263. *Ibid.*
264. Stephen Richardson, personal communication.
265. Janis.
266. U. of Texas.
267. *Ibid.*
268. Mark J. Nearman, *Reactions of a Civilian Population to Threat of Radioactive Contamination,* Committee on Disaster Studies, National Academy of Sciences—National Research Council, 1954 (Unpublished document).
269. Schmideberg.
270. Janis.
271. Schmideberg.
272. U. of Texas.
273. Janis; NORC.
274. Powell.
275. U. of Md.
276. Schmideberg.
277. U. of Md.
278. Schmideberg.
279. Edward Glover, Notes on the Psychological Effects of War Conditions on the Civilian Population (III. The 'Blitz'), *The International Journal of Psychoanalysis, 23,* 1942, pp. 17-36.
280. Janis.
281. NORC.
282. *Ibid.*
283. Janis.
284. U. of Texas.
285. Janis; Powell; Fred C. Ikle, The Effect of War Destruction on the Ecology of Cities, *Social Forces, 29,* 1951, pp. 383-91.
286. Ikle, *op. cit.*
287. *Ibid.*
288. Powell; NORC.
289. U. of Texas.
290. *Ibid.*
291. *Ibid.*
292. *Ibid.*
293. *Ibid.*
294. *Ibid.*
295. NORC.
296. U. of Texas.
297. *Ibid.*
298. *Ibid.*
299. *Ibid.*
300. NORC.
301. *Ibid.*
302. *Ibid.*
303. U. of Md.
304. U. of Texas.
305. *Ibid.*
306. NORC.
307. *Ibid.*
308. U. of Texas.
309. *Ibid.*
310. *Ibid.*
311. *Ibid.*
312. NORC.
313. *Ibid.*
314. U. of Texas.
315. U. of Md.
316. Marie Bonaparte, *op. cit.*
317. Geoffrey Gorer, *The American People,* Norton, New York, 1948.
318. U. of Texas.
319. William James, *Principles of Psychology,* Dover Publications, New York, 1950.
320. NORC.
321. Gorer, *op. cit.*
322. William Caudill, Cultural Perspectives on Stress, *Symposium on Stress,* Army Medical Service Graduate School, Washington, Mar. 1953, pp. 194-208.
323. U. of Md.
324. NORC.
325. *Ibid.*
326. *Ibid.*
327. *Ibid.*
328. U. of Texas.
329. NORC.
330. *Ibid.*
331. Logan, Killian & Marrs, *op. cit.*
332. NORC.
333. U. of Texas.
334. *Ibid.*
335. NORC.

336. U. of Texas.
337. *Ibid.*
338. *Ibid.*
339. NORC.
340. *Ibid.*
341. Norman Cousins, Hiroshima —Four Years Later, *Saturday Review of Literature, 32,* September 17, 1949, pp. 8-10, 30-31.
342. Titmuss, *op. cit.*
343. U. of Texas.
344. *Ibid.*
345. *Ibid.*
346. NORC.
347. *Ibid.*
348. *Ibid.*
349. Colbert & Chamberlin, *op. cit.*
350. Diggory & Pepitone, *op. cit.*
351. Wallace.
352. Nagai, *op. cit.*
353. Bradford B. Hudson, *Observations in a Community during a Flood,* prepared under Navy Contract Nonr-490 (01), Rice Institute (unpublished document); Logan, *Report on England's 1953 Flood Disaster, op. cit.*
354. Powell.
355. U. of Texas.
356. NORC.
357. *Ibid.*
358. *Ibid.*
359. U. of Md.
360. Logan, Killian & Marrs, *op. cit.*
361. *Ibid.;* Powell; NORC.
362. M. Jeanne van Doorn-Janssen, A Study of Social Disorganization in a Community, *Studies in Holland Flood Disaster 1953,* Vol. III, The Institute for Social Research in the Netherlands, Amsterdam, and the National Academy of Sciences—National Research Council, Washington, D. C., 1955, pp. 159-209.
363. Roy A. Clifford, *Informal Group Actions in the Rio Grande Disaster,* A Report to the Committee on Disaster Studies, National Academy of Sciences—National Research

Council, February 1955 (unpublished document).
364. Powell; Wallace.
365. Powell.
366. U. of Texas.
367. Jean Piaget, *The Child's Conception of Physical Causality,* Kegan Paul, London, 1930.
368. Powell.
369. U. of Texas.
370. William James, On Some Mental Effects of the Earthquake, *op. cit.*
371. Sigmund Freud, *Civilization and its Discontents,* Hogarth Press, London, 1949.
372. David P. Boder, personal communication.
373. U. of Md.
374. U. of Texas.
375. John Brooks, A Reporter at Large: Five-ten on a Sticky June Day, *The New Yorker,* May 28, 1955, pp. 39-75.
376. Gorer, *op. cit.*
377. U. of Texas.
378. *Ibid.*
379. NORC.
380. U. of Md.
381. U. of Texas.
382. NORC.
383. *Ibid.*
384. U. of Texas.
385. NORC, *Conference on Field Studies of Reactions to Disaster, op. cit.*
386. Nagai, *op. cit.*
387. Sophocles, *Ajax.*
388. U. of Md.
389. *Ibid.*
390. NORC.
391. Nagai, *op. cit.*
392. Janis, *Psychological Stress, op. cit.*
393. Roy A. Clifford, *op. cit.*
394. Janis.
395. Hersey, *op. cit.*
396. H. R. Veltfort & G. E. Lee, The Cocoanut Grove Fire, A Study in Scapegoating, *Journal of Abnor-*

mal and Social Psychology, 38, 1943, supplement, pp. 138-54.

397. Reports on the disaster of Le Mans in the Paris newspapers: *Le Monde, Combat, Le Figaro, Paris-Presse, France Soir, Franc-Tireur, Observateur,* June 13-30, 1955; unpublished interviews by Charlotte Roland on reactions to the disaster, in Paris, June 1955.

398. Nagai, *op. cit.*

399. Ruth Benedict, *The Chrysanthemum and the Sword,* Houghton Mifflin, Cambridge, Mass., 1946.

400. NORC.

401. U. of Md.

402. *Ibid.*

403. Silone, *op. cit.*

404. Nagai, *op. cit.*

405. NORC.

THE LITERATURE OF DEATH AND DYING

Abrahamsson, Hans. **The Origin of Death:** Studies in African Mythology. 1951

Alden, Timothy. **A Collection of American Epitaphs and Inscriptions with Occasional Notes.** Five vols. in two. 1814

Austin, Mary. **Experiences Facing Death.** 1931

Bacon, Francis. **The Historie of Life and Death with Observations Naturall and Experimentall for the Prolongation of Life.** 1638

Barth, Karl. **The Resurrection of the Dead.** 1933

Bataille, Georges. **Death and Sensuality:** A Study of Eroticism and the Taboo. 1962

Bichat, [Marie François] Xavier. **Physiological Researches on Life and Death.** 1827

Browne, Thomas. **Hydriotaphia.** 1927

Carrington, Hereward. **Death:** Its Causes and Phenomena with Special Reference to Immortality. 1921

Comper, Frances M. M., editor. **The Book of the Craft of Dying and Other Early English Tracts Concerning Death.** 1917

Death and the Visual Arts. 1976

Death as a Speculative Theme in Religious, Scientific, and Social Thought. 1976

Donne, John. **Biathanatos.** 1930

Farber, Maurice L. **Theory of Suicide.** 1968

Fechner, Gustav Theodor. **The Little Book of Life After Death.** 1904

Frazer, James George. **The Fear of the Dead in Primitive Religion.** Three vols. in one. 1933/1934/1936

Fulton, Robert. **A Bibliography on Death, Grief and Bereavement:** 1845-1975. 1976

Gorer, Geoffrey. **Death, Grief, and Mourning.** 1965

Gruman, Gerald J. **A History of Ideas About the Prolongation of Life.** 1966

Henry, Andrew F. and James F. Short, Jr. **Suicide and Homicide.** 1954

Howells, W[illiam] D[ean], et al. **In After Days;** Thoughts on the Future Life. 1910

Irion, Paul E. **The Funeral:** Vestige or Value? 1966

Landsberg, Paul-Louis. **The Experience of Death:** The Moral Problem of Suicide. 1953

Maeterlinck, Maurice. **Before the Great Silence.** 1937

Maeterlinck, Maurice. **Death.** 1912

Metchnikoff, Élie. **The Nature of Man:** Studies in Optimistic Philosophy. 1910

Metchnikoff, Élie. **The Prolongation of Life:** Optimistic Studies. 1908

Munk, William. **Euthanasia.** 1887

Osler, William. **Science and Immortality.** 1904

Return to Life: Two Imaginings of the Lazarus Theme. 1976

Stephens, C[harles] A[sbury]. **Natural Salvation:** The Message of Science. 1905

Sulzberger, Cyrus. **My Brother Death.** 1961

Taylor, Jeremy. **The Rule and Exercises of Holy Dying.** 1819

Walker, G[eorge] A[lfred]. **Gatherings from Graveyards.** 1839

Warthin, Aldred Scott. **The Physician of the Dance of Death.** 1931

Whiter, Walter. **Dissertation on the Disorder of Death.** 1819

Whyte, Florence. **The Dance of Death in Spain and Catalonia.** 1931

Wolfenstein, Martha. **Disaster:** A Psychological Essay. 1957

Worcester, Alfred. **The Care of the Aged, the Dying, and the Dead.** 1950

Zandee, J[an]. **Death as an Enemy According to Ancient Egyptian Conceptions.** 1960